What people are saying about *Nonprofit Strategic Planning...*

Lynne and Linda provide a comprehensive, step-by-step approach to strategic planning. Clear, complete, and concise. A must-have resource for anyone getting ready to start this process.

Thomas Campbell, ACFRE
Vice President for Institutional Advancement
DeSales University

This manual is very well done. I see it as a how-to desktop reference for those who need to stay fresh. It is imperative that fundraisers and nonprofit leaders get this right. It's the building block to the future.

Jay Browning
Associate Vice President for Principal Gifts
University of Cincinnati Foundation

Lynne and Linda have written a comprehensive guide to help nonprofits maximize their potential through strategic planning. Whether large or small, this manual eloquently provides the steps to identify and strategically achieve the goals of an organization to reach its full potential. Required reading for all board members.

Jacqueline Beretta
CEO
TexasNonprofits

I've never read a more useful or practical or reassuring book on strategic planning.

Tom Ahern

The authors have made a major contribution to the strange and challenging journey of strategic planning for nonprofit organizations. This is a must-read for board and key staff. I only wish that I'd had such a comprehensive, easy-to-read resource early on in my career as we struggled with the "product and process." Sidebars are excellent for grounding the content of the subject matter into a reality context that the volunteer board member and paid professional will appreciate. The SWOT tool is an outstanding model on the "how to" of it all. This manual takes the reader through a step-by-step process for a successful three-year plan.

Charles (Chuck) Reynolds
Former Adjunct Faculty, Marywood University and Eastern University Nonprofit
  Master's Program
Emeritus Society Member of the Pennsylvania Association Nonprofit Organizations

If you work with nonprofits, internally or externally, you will benefit from reading this manual. Invaluable information, great step-by-step approach, and takeaways for organizations of all sizes. Especially helpful for new and existing board members.

Susie Schumann
Tax Accountant Specializing in Nonprofit Services
San Antonio, Texas

Nonprofit
Strategic Planning

Develop a Plan That Will Actually Be Used!

Lynne T. Dean, CFRE
Linda Lysakowski, ACFRE

Nonprofit Strategic Planning: Develop a Plan That Will Actually Be Used!

One of the **In the Trenches**™ series

Published by
CharityChannel Press, an imprint of CharityChannel LLC
424 Church Street, Suite 2000
Nashville, TN 37219 USA

CharityChannel.com

In the Trenches, In the Trenches logo, and book design are trademarks of CharityChannel Press, an imprint of CharityChannel LLC.

ISBN Print Book: 978-1-938077-38-8 | ISBN eBook: 978-1-938077-39-5

Library of Congress Control Number: 2015947710

13 12 11 10 9 8 7 6 5 4 3 2 1

Printed in the United States of America

This and most CharityChannel Press books are available at special quantity discounts for bulk purchases for sales promotions, premiums, fundraising, or educational use. For information, contact CharityChannel Press, 424 Church Street, Suite 2000, Nashville, TN 37219 USA. +1 949-589-5938.

About the Authors

Lynne T. Dean, CFRE

Lynne began her career as a journalist and served as reporter and editor for a number of magazines and newspapers. After five years in journalism and public relations, she switched to the nonprofit world and has been working in development for more than twenty years. She has worked for a museum, college, botanical center, and hospital and she currently serves as Director of Institutional Advancement at Northwest Vista College, one of the Alamo Colleges in San Antonio, Texas.

She has also worked as a capital campaign consultant for CCS and Custom Development Solutions before starting her own firm in 2006. Lynne was a key part of the *More than Houses* campaign, which raised more than six hundred million dollars for Habitat for Humanity International. In addition to her work with Habitat affiliates in Dallas, Denver, St. Charles County in Missouri, and Spokane, she has conducted successful fundraising activities and campaigns raising more than $20,000,000 for nonprofits in healthcare, human services, education, and arts and culture.

Lynne received the CFRE designation, a level of recognition obtained by completing training and testing and demonstrating professionalism and talent in the field. She earned a Bachelor's Degree in Psychology from the University of Texas at Austin and has also completed special studies in journalism. In addition to her full-time position, she continues her consulting practice and also provides training and coaching.

She is a contributing author of *You and Your Nonprofit: Practical Advice and Tips from the CharityChannel Professional Community* and an article contributor for CharityChannel. Lynne also serves as an editor for CharityChannel Press and For the Genius Press.

She is immediate past president of the Partnership for Philanthropic Planning San Antonio Chapter and has served on the AFP External Communications Committee and the American Alliance of Museums Development and Membership Standing Committee Executive Board. She serves as CFRE Chair and Employment Opportunities Chair for the AFP San Antonio chapter.

Linda Lysakowski, ACFRE

Linda is one of approximately one hundred professionals worldwide to hold the Advanced Certified Fund Raising Executive designation. Linda had an eleven-year career in banking before entering the nonprofit world. With more than thirty years in the development field, she worked for a university and a museum before starting her own consulting firm. In her twenty-plus years as a philanthropic consultant, Linda has managed capital campaigns that have raised more than $50 million, helped hundreds of nonprofit organizations achieve their development goals, and trained more than thirty thousand development professionals in Canada, Mexico, Egypt, Bermuda, and most of the fifty United States.

A graduate of Alvernia University with majors in Banking and Finance, Theology/Philosophy, and a minor in Communications and AFP's Faculty Training Academy, she is a Master Teacher. Linda is the author of *Recruiting and Training Fundraising Volunteers*; *The Development Plan*; *Fundraising as a Career: What, Are You Crazy?*; *Capital Campaigns: Everything You NEED to Know*; *Are You Ready for a Capital Campaign–The Workbook*; *Raise More Money from Your Business Community*; *Raise More Money from Your Business Community–The Workbook*; *Fundraising for the GENIUS*; a contributing author to *The Fundraising Feasibility Study—It's Not About the Money* and *YOU and Your Nonprofit Board*; co-editor of *YOU and Your Nonprofit* and *The Nonprofit Consulting Handbook;* and co-author of *The Essential Nonprofit Fundraising Handbook* and *The Leaky Bucket: What's Wrong With Your Fundraising… And How You Can Fix It*. In addition to her consulting and training practice, Linda serves as Acquisitions Editor for CharityChannel Press and For the GENIUS Press.

Linda currently serves on the AFP Foundation for Philanthropy Board and on the Professional Advancement Division for AFP, and is past president of the Eastern PA and Sierra (NV) AFP chapters. She has received the Outstanding Fundraiser of the Year award from the Eastern PA, Las Vegas, and Sierra (NV) chapters of AFP.

Authors' Acknowledgments

Lynne T. Dean

I would like to express my deepest appreciation to the nonprofit organizations that make a difference in the lives of individuals and families in our communities. My heartfelt thanks goes especially to those organizations with whom I have worked. It has been and continues to be a pleasure and an honor to have a part in helping each organization move forward in achieving its mission and vision. You are truly heroes and champions.

One special person who has contributed significantly to my personal and professional growth is the founding president of Northwest Vista College, Dr. Jackie Claunch. She brings new meaning to innovation, collaboration, and the "can do" spirit. Thank you, Jackie, for being the amazing person you are.

I would also like to acknowledge my family—Rob, Eric, and Kristin—for their encouragement and support and my great friend Susan for her unwavering belief in my ability to write.

And I want to acknowledge my coauthor, Linda Lysakowski, for having the idea that we should write this manual together. She made it happen, and I have enjoyed working with her and learning from her vast experience in the nonprofit world.

Linda Lysakowski

I would like to acknowledge all the wonderful nonprofit leaders with whom I've done strategic planning. I really enjoyed working with the staff and boards of these groups. There are too many to mention them all, but it's been such a delight to see these organizations moved to a new level after completing a strategic planning process.

I also want to thank some strategic planning facilitators from whom I have learned so much, including Chet Winters, Al Weber, and more.

And I'd especially like to thank my co-author, Lynne Dean, for being such a pleasure to work with and giving me some new insights that I will use in my future planning projects.

Contents

Summary of Chapters

Why Strategic Planning? Whether your nonprofit is small and struggling, in the middle of a growth spurt, or large and well established, you can benefit by looking at the future together as board and staff. In strategic planning, you have a unique opportunity to collaboratively envision your organization's future and determine how to get there. You can take advantage of strategic planning as a tool for changing the mode of functioning from "reactive to proactive." And, such plans are excellent public relations pieces for funders and quite often are required in grant proposals for major projects.

Planning to Plan. There is no single right way for effective strategic planning. You will need to identify and implement the process or way that suits your organization or will best serve your needs. Factors to consider include your resources, engagement of staff and board, internal capacity, and the goals of your organization. You'll need to decide who will manage the process and what the process will look like.

Who Will Participate? Among the important decisions you'll make in strategic planning, your engagement of participants in the process ranks near the top of the list. Quite often, a key board member or the executive director steps into the role of planning process champion and helps to keep the process on track. You will also generally have a plan writer, who will assemble the planning group's decisions into a cohesive document. Additionally, many organizations utilize a planning process facilitator as well as a planning cabinet, which oversees the planning and monitoring of the plan. Other important constituencies include the board, staff, clients, and representatives from key stakeholder groups.

Close Encounters with Assessments, Scans, and Audits. In mapping the future of your organization you will want to better understand the critical issues and opportunities that may have an impact on your mission and vision. An environmental scan is an objective review of the current and anticipated environmental factors such as the political, economic, and demographic environment in which you're operating. Additionally, careful research to identify your strengths and weaknesses, critical issues, external opportunities, current and future challenges, and specific needs of clients and/or members will provide background to the planning team in determining goals and strategies. This situational or SWOT (strengths, weaknesses, opportunities, threats) analysis is derived from your environmental scan. The final piece of the assessment pie is an organization assessment–also commonly referred to as an organizational audit, taking stock, or an information-gathering phase–which lays the groundwork for your strategic plan. As such, it should be conducted very early in the planning process. Its primary purpose is to help stakeholders understand the past and current state of your organization as a launching pad for thinking about the future.

The Planning Retreat. Most planning processes involve one or more half-day, full-day, or two-day retreats during which board, other stakeholders, and staff can come together to work on big-picture themes such as vision, values, and mission, as well as goal-setting. The timing and location of these retreats can make or break the process. This chapter will give you some guidelines to help ensure that your planning retreats add the consensus building and buy-in from all stakeholders.

Values, Mission, and Vision. The words that perplex most nonprofits: *What's the difference between mission and vision—between vision and values? Do we need them all? How do we use them? How do they drive our planning? How long should they be? Who develops them? How often do we need to revisit them, or change them?* All of these questions will be addressed in this chapter.

Goals and Objectives. Many leaders are also perplexed about the difference between goals and objectives, wondering: *Is there a difference? How long a time period should our plan cover? How many goals can we reasonably expect to achieve in this timeframe? How many objectives do we need for each goal?*

Strategies and Tactics (Action Steps). Once you have your goals and objectives, you need strategies for implementing these objectives that will help you achieve your goals. Who is responsible for developing and approving strategies, who implements them? What is the role of the board in developing strategies?

Timelines, Budgets, and Areas of Responsibility. The biggest reason plans don't get implemented is that the planning team has not assigned specific responsibility to an individual or team, a timeline was not set, and/or no budget was established for the strategy. In this chapter you will learn how to answer the key questions—who is going to do it, when is it going to be done, and how much will it cost (or how much needs to be raised?).

Financing the Plan. Here, we will get into more of the details of budgeting and financing your plan. You will get the inside story on how to project human and technology resources that will be necessary to implement your plan.

The Product. Remember, planning is both a process and a product. Both are equally important. We've talked about the process; now let's turn to the product. Who writes the plan? What does it look like? In this chapter we will include sample plan segments and templates so you can develop a plan that works for your organization.

Ensuring Board Buy-In. The board's role in planning is critical to its adoption. Board members should be intimate with the plan's goals and willing to accept responsibility for the things appropriate to the governance role of the board—assuring the board is operating efficiently and legally, recruitment of appropriate board members, oversight of the organization's finances. This chapter will discuss how you can ensure that your board is on board with the plan.

Implementing the Plan. The staff role is making sure the plan gets implemented and understanding the barriers that might prevent full implementation of the plan. This chapter will discuss the importance of developing departmental action plans to assure implementation of the full plan. In particular, we will address the development plan, which is needed to obtain the funding for implementing your goals.

Monitoring and Evaluating the Plan. Okay, the plan is done! Yes! But now, who holds everyone's feet to the fire? The planning cabinet is responsible for periodic evaluation and possible adjustment of the plan as the year progresses. We talk about the role of the cabinet, and implementation benchmarks that will help them monitor the plan.

Planning for the Next Plan. When you monitor and evaluate progress on implementation of the plan throughout the covered time period, you will gain valuable information to use in developing the next plan. As you reach the end of the current planning period, you'll want to closely review all steps in the development and implementation of the existing plan. That close look, a cooperative effort with board members and staff, will help you take advantage of what worked well and minimize the impact of what could have been better. You'll be on the right road to planning for the next plan.

Foreword

The creation of a well-defined, achievable strategic plan is critical to the success of every nonprofit. About a decade ago, I joined the board of a nonprofit that built and ran orphanages in India. Prior to my joining the board, the nonprofit had grown (somewhat sporadically) over time but seemed to drift from one crisis to the next. The first meeting I attended was a day-long strategic planning meeting at the home of a wealthy donor. Although we spent the day having a lovely discussion of a variety of topics related to the agency, we did not create specific measurable strategic goals, an action plan, or anything else which would assist the staff in running the agency. Nothing changed at the agency as a result of that meeting. Over the course of the next year, I worked with the staff to prepare for the next strategic meeting and, at that meeting; we created a strategic plan which had measurable strategic objectives, an action plan, and accountability. Over the course of the next few years, we used the new strategic plan to reorganize the agency, increase funding, and triple the number of orphans we served. Although it can't be said that those results would not have been possible without the new plan, the new strategic plan focused our efforts, aligned the board and staff, and reenergized our organization. That is the power of a well-defined, achievable strategic plan.

Many, if not most, nonprofits today face the same difficulties we had at the Indian orphanage agency. They face an increasingly hostile environment—federal and state budget cutbacks, increased demand for services, very competitive fundraising dynamics, and government regulation. The challenges they encounter require them to be both nimble and strategic. Unfortunately, most agencies find it difficult to plan because they are immersed in the hectic day-to-day activities of running an agency or they lack the experience and know-how to conduct strategic planning. As a result, it is virtually impossible for them to consistently respond to everyday crises or operate strategically.

Lynne Dean and Linda Lysakowski's new manual, *Nonprofit Strategic Planning: Develop a Plan That Will Actually Be Used!*, arms nonprofits with the tools they need to create a plan to both define, and achieve their missions. Their manual outlines, in detail, each of the tasks necessary to create a comprehensive, executable strategic plan—choosing the committee, performing the organizational audit, planning a retreat, clarifying mission and vision, establishing an action plan as well as each of the other steps in the process.

To me, it was equally important that the authors shared with their readers a series of what I would call the "Big Questions." These questions cover everything from the meeting planning process to the questions which must be reflected upon to understand an agency's core values. I found the question positing process to be a vital part of their work because, when used properly, their questions will enable staffs and boards to begin the critical conversations from which a proper strategic plan will emerge.

Although each of the steps of the strategic process is important, the creation of vision and mission is a pivotal part of the strategic planning process. This part of the process can elevate or derail the entire plan. As described in **Chapter Six**, the creation of a mission statement guides the agency's daily work, keeps the agency from drifting into projects that are tangential to its true purpose and guides the development of the strategic plan. This section of the work is a great example of where the questioning process introduced by the authors is so important. The mission questions prescribed by the authors will enable any strategic planning committee to dig deeply into its agency's work and emerge with a crisp, clear rendition of the agency's mission. The agency's vision, on the other hand, is loftier and pictures the world as it might be if the agency achieved its mission. It inspires the daily work of the agency and focuses the goal-setting work of strategic planning. Once again, the authors offer us a series of questions that will enable an agency to create an inspiring vision.

One of the major challenges in strategic planning is the tendency in busy organization leaders to take thoughtful, well-written strategic plans and place them on a shelf in a prominent place in their office where they sit and gather dust. I was pleased that the authors provided a road map for organizations to put their plans into practice by helping the reader create SMART (Specific, Measurable, Action-oriented, Realistic, and Time-defined) Strategic Objectives (**Chapter Seven**) and create tactical action plans (**Chapter Eight**) which clearly define the tactics/actions necessary to implement the strategic plan, the person or team responsible for the assigned action step, and a target date for completion. The importance of this part of the strategic planning process cannot be over emphasized. The SMART Strategic Objectives and tactical action plans give both the board and the staff scorecards from which the entire organization can hold itself accountable. This is critical if an agency wants to get serious about implementing its strategic plan. At our Foundation, we publish a monthly scorecard that measures our progress on the implementation of our strategic objectives. The scorecard outlines strategic objectives for each department and the Foundation itself and assigns a red, yellow or green signal to illustrate our progress. We believe that it encourages us to be accountable and allows for transparency throughout the Foundation.

Nonprofit Strategic Planning: Develop a Plan That Will Actually Be Used! gives agency leaders the tools they needs to create a robust strategic road map to guide their everyday decision making and long-term strategy. I highly recommend it for any nonprofit beginning its strategic planning journey.

Dennis Noll
CEO, San Antonio Area Foundation

Introduction

Okay, we know—you'd love to do strategic planning but who has the time? You're running a nonprofit, working lean and mean. You're overworked and understaffed. You're busy serving your mission. Your clients come first. Your board doesn't want to get bogged down in meeting after meeting to plan for the future. We need to deal with today!

What, you say you wouldn't love to do strategic planning? You've been there, done that, and have the battle scars to prove it. You have a dandy plan that is somewhere in your office—let's see now, where was that plan again?

Oh darn, those pesky funders are asking to see your plan. Well, I guess if we have to do it, let's get it over as quickly and painlessly as possible.

Oh wait, those clients that come first—have you really thought about *their* future? And those board members that don't want to take time to plan—do they *really* understand your mission and vision? And those staff people who are so overworked—could you make their job easier and their work time more productive?

Hmm, maybe this planning idea isn't so bad after all. But—how can I do it while balancing all my other work?

We've been there and done this ourselves. This is why we wrote the manual—to let you know you can do it, too. You can develop a plan that works. You can get people in your organization not only willing, but enthused, about writing the plan, and you can implement the plan to bring abut change in your organization.

Turn the page and let's get started.

Chapter One

Why Strategic Planning?

IN THIS CHAPTER

···→ Changing from reactive to proactive

···→ Developing a common vision

···→ Increasing sustainability

Whether you and your nonprofit are small and struggling, in the middle of a growth spurt, or large and well established, you can benefit by looking at the future together as board and staff.

In strategic planning, you have a unique opportunity to collaboratively envision your organization's future and determine how to get there. You can take advantage of strategic planning as a tool for changing the mode of functioning from "reactive to proactive." And, such plans help get everyone moving forward toward a common destination or vision and have a positive impact on the sustainability of your organization. And, not exactly coincidently, these plans make excellent public relations pieces for funders and quite often you'll notice them as a required item or reference in grant proposals for major projects.

Changing From Reactive to Proactive

Everyone from fictional characters such as the Cheshire Cat in Alice in Wonderland to well-known and even some not so well-known thinkers of our time tell us the importance of knowing where you are going. Our favorite sage advice comes from the succinct lines of Steve Maraboli, author of *Life, the Truth and Being Free*. He poses the thought-provoking question, "if you don't know exactly where you are going, how will you know when you get there?"

What you don't want your organization to be faced with is that proverbial fork in the road, and trying to take it—going all directions at the same time. Or, as they say, fixing the plane while you're flying.

> *When you get to a fork in the road, take it.*
>
> —Yogi Berra

Linda was hired to provide some training and technical assistance to a group of organizations throughout the United States that had one thing in common—they were all recipients of a very large federal grant that provided the majority of funding for many of these nonprofits. Alas, one day the funding agency said, "Guess what folks, we are no longer funding you!" In Linda's work with these groups she found that a number of them were totally reactive—they panicked when their funding was cut and quickly tried to recover by developing plans to diversify their funding streams. Unfortunately for some of these agencies it was too late. If they had been proactive and developed a strategic plan before this crisis hit, many of them would still be thriving today. The reality was that some of them folded the program which this funding had supported, and a few—for whom this was their only program—closed their doors altogether. Lesson learned: don't wait until it's too late, plan now!

 **stories from the real world**

So, does your nonprofit organization need a road map, or a GPS (global positioning system) for navigating its future? We can say with a substantial degree of certainty that the road map or GPS you've created through your strategic plan will help you discover a major benefit of strategic planning. But even more than providing direction and guidance, a strategic plan can take you away from the land of quick fixes and reactive management and operations to a better place characterized by proactive management in day-to-day activities.

We've noticed that many nonprofits have a tendency to plan and run at the same time and, generally speaking, the results are not too pretty. Quick fixes just seem to add to the pressure of accomplishing the greater good. Scrambling for a solution, wiping sweat off your brow, exhaling while you work—does that sound familiar? We hope not.

Is your organization reactive? The reactive approach or quick fixes can be costly and you may have a tendency to overlook important details.

Or would you say that your operational style is more proactive? Now is the time to raise your hand to say you'll join the ranks of proactive organizations. Once you take this important step, you will be joining the growing number of nonprofits who are taking the time and making the investment in strategic planning. Think about it. Doesn't it just make sense to spend a little time and money up front in planning than trying to fix problems which seem to pop up over and over again?

Developing a Common Vision

Close your eyes and try to imagine the differing ideas and perspectives that various stakeholders have about your organization's future. Does your board think about the future the same way your staff thinks about it? What about your clients and consumers? And, what do your funders, supporters, and even potential funders have to say about your future?

We have good news for you. Your completed strategic plan can integrate these diverse perspectives into a well-crafted vision of your organization's future. No matter how large the differences may seem among your various stakeholders, you will find that this diverse group

An organization serving victims of abuse had an array of programs and services tailored to meet the needs of victims. But they believed they could do much more. So they developed a series of educational programs for students at the college, high school, and middle school level. The programs engaged students in recognizing potentially abusive behaviors and identifying ways to help prevent abuse. This educational and proactive approach has increased awareness of abuse in the community and has added an important program component to the way this agency fulfills its mission. And, it all began because they wanted to be more proactive.

 **stories from the real world**

can play a significant, even vital role in your planning process. They will have an opportunity to be heard. They will bring differing perspectives and ideas on everything from organizational resources to potential obstacles to priority action areas. And, believe it or not, your organization will benefit by listening and working through these widely varying viewpoints.

For example, we see organizations struggling with board members who have different ideas than staff members. Rather than limit the planning process to only board members or only staff members, most organizations find it helpful and refreshing to bring everyone together, recognize differences, and even incorporate some of these varying views into the process.

The end product—or your shared vision—will reflect the culmination of your work together throughout the planning process and will enable each contributor to "have ownership" and feel a part of its creation. Another benefit of this inclusive approach is that you and your stakeholders may discover an exciting energy and enthusiasm for moving forward on identifying the path to achieving that desired future.

Increasing Sustainability

Strategic plans are the basis for department action plans:

- Development plan
- Program plan
- Facilities plan
- Marketing plan
- Governance plan
- Financial plan

Strategic planning often lays the groundwork for development planning and these two levels of planning have a major impact on the sustainability of an organization. Before we go any further, though, we want to emphasize that your strategic plan should not simply say what your funders want you to say to get funding or be a response to an item in a grant application. Remember the importance of diverse perspectives we talked about earlier?

We all agree that funding has significant impact on sustainability. And a successful development plan will generally start with the strategic plan and then add such elements as the case for support and an outline of how donors will be identified, cultivated, and asked to give.

But sustainability really includes more than organizational funding. Sustainability also relates to the programs and services your nonprofit provides or seeks to provide. Throughout the planning process, your organization and your stakeholders have the opportunity to look at what you do, or its particular service niche, as well as funding strategies for ensuring that you can manage and operate those services.

In addition to closely reviewing your organization's current areas of service, the participants in your planning process may also identify areas of service that can be changed if funds are lacking. They may also pinpoint service areas that might benefit if more funding becomes available. You can thus directly connect strategic planning to sustainability in programs and services and have more clarity as you make critical decisions in the future.

One organization had developed a five-year strategic plan that covered all its program areas, a forecasted expansion, and a staffing and volunteer plan. When it came time to raise the money for the planned expansion, the campaign consultant was able to draw most of the information for the case for support from the strategic plan. Because the organization had a solid plan in place, it was able to save countless hours and a good deal of money to build its capital campaign case statement.

Example

So, yes, you can certainly develop and include information required on grant applications and proposals about planning. But this information really shouldn't be a substitute for the strategic planning process. You will need a case for support, but often the case can be developed by building on the strategic plan.

Maybe your organizational budget includes restricted funds that are tied to a specific donor's requirements. These restrictions, however, should not define or be part of your overall strategy. We emphasize here and throughout this manual that strategic planning is a process. And, yes, that process is different for different organizations.

To Recap

◆ The culmination of that process, your strategic plan, just like a road map, shows the pathway your entire organization will travel on the road to its shared vision of the future.

◆ That road map will also help you identify the characteristics of programs and activities that are the right fit for your mission and vision.

◆ Ultimately, your strategic plan should increase your organization's odds for impact and sustainability.

Chapter Two

Planning to Plan

IN THIS CHAPTER

---→ Are you committed to the planning process?

---→ Who will manage the process?

---→ What will the process look like?

While there is no single right way for effective strategic planning, there is one thing all good plans have in common—the people designing those plans were committed to creating a plan that would work. Although the plans for different organizations might look different, they all have one thing in common—they are both a process and a product. In this chapter, we talk about the *process* of planning.

You will need to identify and implement the process in the way that suits your organization or will best serve your needs. Factors to consider include your resources, engagement of staff and board, internal capacity, and the goals of your organization. Some people are really great at process, they love the research, the consensus-building, the brainstorming. However, sometimes process-oriented people lack the ability to develop the *product*—the actual written plan. Be careful when you develop your process to keep the end product in mind. You'll need to decide who will manage the process and what the process and the product will look like.

Who Will Manage the Process?

One of the first steps is to decide who is going to manage the planning process and who will be involved. As we said in **Chapter One**, the board and staff should both be involved in the process in order for it to be effective. So, who takes the lead? In larger organizations, we've found that typically planning is a staff-driven process. It is usually the executive director in a larger organization who gets the ball rolling. The director might then appoint a planning cabinet, consisting of board and staff members. Key staff members, such as program administrators, the director of development, or the chief financial officer might serve on this cabinet.

In a smaller organization, the process might be led by the board. Often the vice chair of the board is responsible for guiding the planning process, since the implementation of the plan will most likely take place during the incoming chair's term in office. Again a planning cabinet composed of staff and board members might be appointed to guide the planning process. Board committee chairs might be asked to serve on this committee since the plan will affect the work of the committees.

You might also want to include some community representatives on your planning cabinet: major donors, volunteers, clients, community leaders.

In most cases, an outside consultant, or facilitator, is used to manage the process. The planning consultant will work with the cabinet to plan the process. If the board and staff are experienced at planning, they might do most of the pre-planning and prepare the planning document, but use a facilitator to conduct the planning retreat(s).

On our planning cabinet we will include:

◆ Our executive director

◆ The following board members:

_____

_____

_____

◆ The following staff members:

_____

_____

_____

◆ Other committee members:

_____

_____

_____

to-do lists

So perhaps before we go any farther, why not decide who in your organization should serve on the planning cabinet.

You should also decide early on in the process what level of involvement you will need from a consultant or facilitator.

Answer these questions:

◆ Do we want someone to do an external analysis (i.e., demographic study)?

◆ Do we need someone to prepare the planning document?

◆ Do we need someone to design assessment templates or surveys?

◆ Do we need someone to facilitate a retreat(s)?

What Will the Process Look Like?

Usually the process begins with an assessment of where you are now. Do you have a strategic plan in place already? If so, it needs to be reviewed to determine which goals have been completed,

---

Appreciative Inquiry—A way to examine and analyze developmental change, created by David Cooperrider and Suresh Srivastva at Case Western Reserve Weatherhead School of Management in the 1980s. This system puts the spotlight on the best in an organization and uses provocative questions, storytelling, and directed conversation.

Development Audit—An objective evaluation, sometimes conducted by professional fundraising counsel, of an organization's internal development procedures and results, according to the Association of Fundraising Professional's Fundraising Dictionary.

Feasibility Study—An objective survey, usually conducted by fundraising counsel, of an organization's fundraising potential. The study assesses the strength of the organization's case and the availability of its leaders, workers and prospective donors. The written report includes the study findings, conclusions, and recommendations, according to the AFP Fundraising Dictionary.

definition

which ones are still valid, and which are no longer pertinent.

In **Chapter Four** we will talk more about the SWOT analysis and about ways to assess your internal strengths and weaknesses and your external opportunities and threats. This is one of the most widely used assessment tools, but there are others such as appreciative inquiry, conducting surveys, development audits and other organizational audits, and feasibility studies. Depending on the level of sophistication your organization needs, whether or not you've done any type of assessment already, what your budget is for planning, and what timeline you are on, you will need to decide which of these assessment methods is appropriate for your organization.

When talking to facilitators or consultants, be sure you understand the full rate they're charging. For example, do their fees include:

◆ Travel (mileage or rental car, airfare, hotels, transportation to and from airports, preparation time, etc.)?

◆ Phone calls?

◆ Materials?

observation

Also part of the process is gaining stakeholder input. This will be discussed in more detail in **Chapter Four**, but again, you will need to take the methods for accomplishing this step into consideration when laying out your timeline and budget for planning.

In most cases there will be at least one board/staff retreat, possibly several full-day planning sessions. You will find it helpful to get people away from their usual work environment so they can focus on planning. This is not something that can be accomplished solely through staff and board meetings. These meetings will most likely require a facilitator, so early in your planning process you should determine who will provide the meeting facilitation and how much it will cost, including venue charges and travel expenses if you work with an out-of-town consultant.

To Recap

◆ Planning to plan is an important first step.

◆ You will need to determine the process you will follow before establishing a budget and timeline for planning.

◆ Planning requires both time and money to do it right.

Chapter Three

Who Will Participate

IN THIS CHAPTER

···➤ Who are your stakeholders?

···➤ Recruiting the planning cabinet

···➤ Clarifying roles and expectations

Among the important decisions you'll make in strategic planning, your engagement of participants in the process ranks near the top of the list. Quite often, a key board member or the executive director steps into the role of planning process champion and helps to keep the process on track. You will also generally have a plan writer, who will assemble the planning group's decisions into a cohesive document.

Additionally, many organizations utilize a planning process facilitator as well as a planning cabinet, which oversees the planning and monitoring of the plan. Important constituencies you will want to participate include the board, staff, clients, and representatives from key stakeholder groups.

Who Are Your Stakeholders?

Gaining a clear understanding of what your organization's stakeholders need and how to address those needs represents a key element of success in strategy development. The term "stakeholder" for our purposes refers to someone who has an interest or concern in your organization or its work. Your stakeholders can include donors, staff members, board members, clients, volunteers, and the general public.

Each stakeholder group has specific needs and expectations and can be internal or external to your agency. So, it's easy to see that with all these diverse stakeholder groups, often having conflicting needs and expectations, how important it is that you take the time to prioritize and focus on voices that should be heard in the planning process.

As you develop your list of potential stakeholders, you may want to divide the list into two segments— direct and intermediary stakeholders.

Direct stakeholders include:

◆ Funders

◆ Board members

◆ Staff

◆ Clients or those who benefit from your services

Example

Direct stakeholders are those with a direct connection to your organization.

Intermediary stakeholders are those who represent others. They may still have an interest in you, but that interest will be different than the interest that a direct stakeholder has.

Recruiting the Planning Cabinet

An important part of organizing the planning process is determining who will oversee the process and serve on the leadership group or planning cabinet. This group will also make final decisions concerning the direction of the plan. Throughout the process, they will meet to receive information, provide input, and make decisions. Preparing a job description which you can discuss with potential cabinet members will help clarify the role and responsibilities of this group as you recruit its members.

So, who should be included in this leadership group? Typically, this group ranges in size from ten to fifteen members, although for smaller organizations a workable group may include four to seven members. You will want to consider your organization's culture and politics when you determine who should serve on this committee. You'll also need to have representatives from groups that must approve the plan for your strategic plan to have the optimal chance for successful implementation.

What about including board members in this leadership group? Absolutely! Yes, the entire board will approve the strategic plan and monitor performance against the plan; however, individual board members can play larger roles in the process by serving on the planning cabinet.

Ideally, your planning cabinet will include a planning champion from your board of directors—that person on the board who has a passion for planning and is willing to do whatever it takes to develop a strategic plan and follow the plan through its implementation.

Strive to recruit members of the planning cabinet from key stakeholders or constituents who will be affected by the plan. Membership should be open to both board members and non-board members and the executive director or CEO should also serve as a voting member of the cabinet.

Clarifying Roles and Expectations

Strategic planning involves a number of various groups, stakeholders, and/or constituents. The varying groups contribute in a number of ways and participation by some groups may overlap with others.

Let's start with the role of the board. Board members can and should be involved in every step of the process. Individual board members may choose to participate in different ways and at various levels. No matter the level of involvement, an organization's strategic plan is ultimately "owned" by the board

Intermediary stakeholders (or indirect stakeholders) include:

◆ City or county government agencies

◆ The wider community or parents of children in the community

◆ The media

◆ Community and local foundations

◆ Donors

◆ Local businesses

Example

Planning Cabinet Job Description

◆ Oversee and help move the process forward

◆ Meet routinely throughout the planning process to receive information and provide input

◆ Make key strategy and financial decisions

◆ Approve the planning document prior to submitting for board approval

Example

---

of directors. We emphasize here that the most important role of the board is approval of the strategic plan. The board will also play a leading role in monitoring performance against the plan.

Of course, throughout the process, board members can participate more actively by doing such tasks from helping to plan the process to working on framing the strategic questions they would like answered during the process.

Willing board members might, armed with a set of strategic questions, interview key stakeholders or others with critical and valuable information. By engaging board members in this way, organizations may build personal investment in the plan by those board members conducting the interviews, help develop stakeholder support, help strengthen essential relationships, and increase board member knowledge.

The members of the leadership group or planning cabinet oversee the process and makes strategy and financial decisions. During their meetings they review data, look at key information identified, and make decisions about goals, strategies, and metrics. They share information and discuss the implications of information for strategic plan elements. And, quite often, they discuss more than one element of the plan at each meeting.

One organization gained input from its stakeholders by using surveys designed by the consultant engaged for that purpose. The groups surveyed included board, staff, volunteers, and other agencies in the community. The consultant also met face-to-face with representatives of these groups as well as an Ambassador's Council which advised the organization. The plan was successfully implemented because the organization included the right input from the right people.

Example

Representatives from identified stakeholder groups participate in the strategic planning process by providing their perspectives and input regarding the community and the environment in which the organization operates. Although staff members, as key stakeholders, participate in various phases of the process, their primary role and more active part in the plan centers on providing input about implementation.

To Recap

◆ A planning process thrives on energetic cooperation among board members, leadership, staff, and other stakeholders.

◆ A planning cabinet consisting of about ten to fifteen members should be invited to serve as the leadership group for the process and to make the tough decisions as you navigate through the planning.

◆ When you involve stakeholders and ensure that everyone understands their roles and what to expect during the process, you and your organization will be promoting buy-in for the plan. And, you'll have a group of empowered and enthusiastic participants who can provide the momentum needed to advance the planning agenda.

Chapter Four

Close Encounters with Assessments, Scans, and Audits

IN THIS CHAPTER

···➔ How and when to do a SWOT analysis

···➔ Do you need an environmental scan?

···➔ Do you need a full-blown organizational assessment?

In mapping the future of your organization, you will want to better understand the critical issues and opportunities that may have an impact on your mission and vision. An environmental scan is an objective review of the current and anticipated environmental factors such as the political, economic, and demographic environment in which you're operating.

Additionally, careful research to identify your strengths and weaknesses, critical issues, external opportunities, current and future challenges, and specific needs of clients and/or members will provide background to the planning team in determining goals and strategies. This situational or SWOT (strengths, weaknesses, opportunities, threats) analysis is derived from your environmental scan.

The final piece of the assessment pie is an organization assessment–also commonly referred to as an organizational audit, taking stock, or an information-gathering phase–which lays the groundwork for your strategic plan. As such, this assessment should be conducted very early in the planning process. Its primary purpose is to help stakeholders understand the past and current state of your organization as a launching pad for thinking about the future.

> ### Organizational Audit or Assessment
>
> This type of tool is an internal analysis on the quality of the most important practices in your organization. Categories you may wish to assess include governance, human resources, programs, finance, and fundraising. A free online assessment is available at www.surveymonkey.com/s.asp?u=3754722401. This survey is provided by Authenticity Consulting, LLC, and is used with permission from the Greater Twin Cities United Way.
>
>

The Environmental Scan

If this is the first time you are doing a strategic plan, if it has been more than five to seven years since you did a plan, or if your community environment has drastically changed since you last did a plan, you will most likely need an environmental scan of your community before you can determine whether your goals are relevant and doable.

Who Does This Scan

Although your planning cabinet can help conduct interviews, this scan should be led by a professional consultant who will know what information is relevant and where to find it. Some types of information you might find useful include:

◆ Is your community growing or shrinking in size?

◆ How are the demographics of your community shifting, in regard to age, ethnicity, socioeconomic status?

◆ What are your current community needs?

◆ Who is currently meeting those needs (competition perhaps)?

◆ Are there unmet needs in the community?

◆ What government or government-funded resources are available in your community?

◆ Are there organizations with which you can partner to deliver needed services?

Resources for External Information

Educational: U.S. Department of Education, National Center for Education Statistics (NCES) for student enrollments

Demographic: U.S. Department of Labor, Bureaus of Labor Statistics (BLS) for information on labor market forecasts; also state and local Departments of Labor, Commerce or Business Development for information on the workforce and education levels

Political/governmental: State and local employment statutes, Internet and political trend watchers, national and local newspapers, news magazines (i.e., Wall Street Journal)

Economic/social/cultural: U.S. Department of Labor, National Association of State Personnel Executives, Federal Deposit Insurance Corporation, national and local newspapers, news magazines for unemployment rates, emerging occupations and competencies, prevalence of outsourcing or privatization, availability of affordable housing, transportation, and health care

Geographic: U.S. Department of Labor, National Center for Health Statistics for migration patterns, desirability of key geographic areas

Technology: News reports and magazines, Internet searches on technology trends, technology watch groups such as TrendHunter (trendhunter.com), U.S. Department of Health and Social Services for emerging trends in technology and the types of skills needed for new technology

Example

Internal Information

◆ Employee skills and competencies; training programs offered and attended

◆ Employee demographics: number of full- and part-time employees; diversity; retirement eligibility

◆ Labor relations: organization's relationship with unions; current labor agreement provisions and expiration dates

◆ Organizational climate: experience with change; staff feeling supported or overwhelmed

◆ Turnover: types of turnover, the amount, and reasons for leaving

◆ Leadership: possible changes

◆ Budget: available funds for new positions, salary increases, training, technology

Most of this information may be obtained from Human Resources staff and internal reports such as budget and financial reports.

Example

◆ What is the current political environment you're facing and how will it affect your services?

◆ Are there potential untapped funding sources for your organization?

A skilled consultant can collect lots of information about your community through online resources and/or through interviews with key community leaders. If your budget is limited, you might ask the consultant to design the questionnaire and send your planning cabinet members out to do the interviews. Or you might ask the consultant for a list of needed information and ask one of your planning cabinet members who is skilled in research to find the answers through searching websites and online information. It is amazing what is available online.

There are also a number of things you can find inside your own organization. This is why it's important to include staff in the planning process. While the entire staff might not serve on the planning cabinet or attend a planning retreat, you should involve them in evaluating the strengths, weaknesses, opportunities, and threats of your organization.

The SWOT Analysis:

You are probably familiar with the term—SWOT—which stands for strengths, weaknesses, opportunities, and threats. Where a lot of people go astray is trying to categorize items into strengths or opportunities, and weaknesses or threats. The first step in remembering what the difference is to understand what each of these terms means.

Some examples of strengths might be:

◆ We have a board that understands its role of governance.

◆ Our CEO had been with the organization for fifteen years and is well respected in the community.

◆ We have a diverse stream of funding sources.

◆ We have a staff that is well-trained.

Some examples of weaknesses might be:

◆ We do not have working committees on our board.

◆ Our staff is stretched too thin; we do not have enough staff members.

Strengths and *weaknesses* are internal to the organization.

Opportunities and *threats* are external to the organization.

 finition

◆ We rely exclusively on grants and special events for funding.

◆ We do not have a formal volunteer program.

On the other hand, looking at external resources, some examples of opportunities might include:

◆ Several new companies have moved into our community; these companies could be a source of funding and volunteers for our agency.

◆ Our board has untapped connections to the philanthropic community.

◆ There are several agencies doing different work but in our area of service, with which we might partner to provide services.

◆ We have a lot of enthused parents of clients that could be tapped to form a young professionals group.

And, some examples of threats might include:

◆ Our major funder has recently merged with another company, also a funder, eliminating a key source of funding for us.

◆ Our community is becoming more diverse (the corresponding weakness might be that we are not equipped to handle the language issues associated with this diversity).

◆ A major source of county government funding is likely to end with a new administration.

◆ The economy has affected our community adversely.

Another issue many groups have is trying to be realistic about the strengths and weaknesses, as well as the opportunities and threats. We have found that in most cases as we lead a group through the SWOT exercise, everyone is enthused about listing the strengths of the organization and often very optimistic about the opportunities but this same group is reluctant to discuss weaknesses and threats. This is one of the major reasons you need a trained facilitator to lead this session who can work with the group to realistically assess its internal and external environment.

The Organizational Assessment

Lynne worked with a conservation organization which used a SWOT analysis as part of its strategic planning. The answers revealed that the organization did not have enough events and activities throughout the year to increase awareness of their mission and attract more visitors to its site. As a result of that discovery, that nonprofit included an expanded focus on educational, on-site learning activities for a range of age levels at different times in the year as one of the goals in its strategic plan.

Example

What the environmental scan does to more fully explore the opportunities and threats, an organizational assessment, or audit, does to examine more closely the internal strengths and weaknesses of the organization. Often before a plan can be done, you will need a full-blown internal assessment.

You will probably not need to do these audits on an annual basis as you would your financial audit, but it is a good idea to consider doing them every five years or so, when you are preparing your strategic plan.

Unlike the external environmental scan, which can utilize your planning cabinet, these audits should always be done by outside consultants. It is very difficult, if not impossible, for you to evaluate your internal strengths on your own. As we've mentioned in the SWOT Analysis section, it is usually very hard for organizations to step back and realistically look at their internal operations, especially the weaknesses.

When looking for outside experts to help you with this organizational assessment, you will most likely want to engage a team of experts—one that is an expert in financial development, one whose area of expertise is in human resources, one who is a governance expert, a program expert, and an architect or facilities manager who can realistically assess your facility needs.

One organization before completing its strategic plan, engaged several consultants to do internal audits—a development audit, a human resources audit, a governance audit, a program audit, and a facilities audit, in addition to the normal financial audit that all organizations do each year. These audits formed a good basis for planning because the organization understood very realistically what it was facing.

Example

Do We Need All of These Assessments and Scans?

Most likely the answer is yes. Of course, if you have recently done some of these assessments, the information is probably still valid. If it's been five years or more, you will probably need updated assessments.

Sometimes, if your budget is very small, or time is of the essence, you can accomplish a lot just through the SWOT analysis which is typically done in a board/staff retreat environment during the planning process. But, in most cases, an in-depth plan requires the internal organization assessment and the environmental scans early on in the planning process. These can then be reviewed and expanded on during the SWOT Analysis. It is usually impossible to tackle all of the areas of concern in one plan, so you might want to do the organization assessment and the environmental scan and then choose priorities during the SWOT Analysis in order to decide which items should be part of this current plan.

To Recap

◆ The SWOT Analysis as part of the planning process looks at internal strengths and weaknesses and external opportunities and threats.

◆ A more in-depth look at external factors is done through an environmental scan which helps you review your community needs before planning how you can address these needs.

◆ An organizational assessment, or audit, will help you analyze your integral strengths and weaknesses in all areas-governance, staffing, volunteers, facility, funding, and programs.

Chapter Five

The Planning Retreat

IN THIS CHAPTER

◆ Is a retreat really necessary?

◆ How long does a retreat last?

◆ Where and when should the retreat be held?

◆ Who should attend?

◆ Who should lead the retreat?

Okay, we know what you're thinking! "Our board is sick of retreats, they just want to get the plan done." "We cannot afford the time or money to do a retreat." "We don't need a facilitator, we can do a retreat ourselves." "Do we really want to 'retreat' from our planning duties?"

A few years ago, it became quite popular to refer to the annual board retreat as a "board advance" in order to put a more positive spin on the process. After all, we want our board to advance don't we, not to retreat from its duties?

Yes, we do want the process to help advance our mission, our vision, our programs. But, we still like the term—board retreat. Here's why.

The retreat is an occasion to get your board and staff away from your usual meeting space, to take the time to really think about where the organization is going and how it will get there, and to get to know each other better. So retreat, rather than being a negative word, can be almost like a spiritual retreat—a time to take stock, to be inspired, and to move towards a more positive future.

So is the retreat a necessary part of the planning process. We think, yes!

How Long Should the Retreat Last?

As long as you need! Okay, that might be too broad an answer. We find that most groups need at least two sessions in order to get everything done. Sometimes groups opt for a two-day retreat, maybe a

One organization decided its board would just not take the time to do a planning retreat, so the executive director decided to "back into" the planning process by presenting the board with a staff-developed mission and vision statement, get their approval, and then present the staff-determined goals for the next year. After this process was completed, it would be easy to get the board to buy into implementing the goals. But what really happened? The board did not have buy-in, and said to the executive director, "sure these goals look good—go implement them."

stories from the real world

Friday evening and Saturday morning. Others do an intensive all-day retreat, perhaps all day on Saturday if most of the board members cannot get away during the week.

Ideally, the first session is held to solidify mission, vision, and values, and to determine goals. After giving the planning cabinet an opportunity to review what was accomplished at the first session, a second session is held a few weeks later. Sometimes even a third session is necessary.

Where and When Should the Retreat Be Held?

A retreat should be exactly what the name implies—a getaway from your normal routine. A place to step back and look at your organization with fresh eyes. Timing will depend on the schedules of board and staff members and possibly other stakeholder groups you might want to invite to at least part of your retreat. You may, for example, want to invite community members to come in and help you conduct the SWOT analysis. Fresh eyes and fresh ideas from people not intimately connected to your organization help shed light on areas you might not think are important, but which the community feels are vital aspects of your programs.

One organization that served adults with developmental disabilities, for example, invited parents of the people they served to come in and talk about what they saw as the strengths, weaknesses, opportunities,

---

One organization that completed a successful planning process held a first session at which the following things were accomplished:

◆ Mission, vision, and values were reviewed and adjustments were suggested

◆ SWOT analysis was completed

◆ Review of the previous plan was done

◆ Preliminary goals and objectives were established

◆ Work groups based on the three major goals were appointed and assigned work to be completed before the next retreat.

The second retreat was held a few weeks later. At this session, the following tasks were completed:

◆ Revised mission, vision, and values were approved.

◆ Strategies were developed to implement objectives.

◆ Preliminary timelines, budgets, and areas of responsibilities were assigned.

After the second retreat, the facilitator and staff prepared the first draft of the plan, which was then reviewed and adjusted by each work group, resulting in a final plan.

Example

and threats of the organization. The input of these parents was invaluable in helping the organization craft its plan.

If yours is a national or international organization, scheduling might be a bit more challenging. We've been involved with several national and international groups that held a special planning session before one of their regular board meetings, since getting people together for another special session would be challenging due to costs and travel time.

Location, Location, Location

Where to hold your retreat? As we've said, not in your office, please!!!

We've done retreats in interesting locations such as:

- A museum
- A country club
- A bird sanctuary
- A board member's office suite
- An environmental center
- An arboretum
- A hotel
- Poolside at a board member's home

> Do not attempt to do planning at a regular board meeting. There are too many other items of business that need to get done, and too many distractions such as board members arriving late, leaving early, staff members being sidetracked by routine office duties, and staff being interrupted by other staff members.
>
>
> ❗ important

You might even plan an outing along with the retreat, and invite spouses of staff and board members to attend the social part of the retreat. One group, for example, held its retreat at a museum, and asked the museum director to take the participants and their spouses on a private tour of the museum after the session. Another group arranged a tour of local historic sites for spouses while the board and staff was tied up in the retreat, and then everyone had dinner together.

Who Should Attend?

Your planning cabinet will ultimately decide who should attend the retreat, but at the very least it should include:

- The entire board
- Executive staff

> One group had a half-day morning retreat for staff members, followed by a joint lunch, and then an afternoon session for its board members. Work groups of board and staff were assigned to work together on certain goals after the first session, and a second session was held with board and staff together.
>
> **Example**

You might also have all staff involved in portions of the retreat as well as other stakeholders. You will not want these groups to be part of the entire process, as larger groups tend to get unwieldy, and sometimes the "dirty laundry" needs to get aired at these sessions.

Some groups have invited various stakeholders groups to attend, such as parents, community leaders, and other nonprofits with whom the agency partners. These people will likely not want to take part in the nitty-gritty planning process, but can be helpful in determining the organization's strengths and weaknesses.

Who Should Lead the Retreat?

You need a facilitator. Yes, it will likely cost you some money. Yes, the facilitator might not know your organization inside out. But the objectivity of an outside facilitator is essential. You also need someone who can keep the group on track. Perhaps you have an experienced facilitator within your organization and you're tempted to use that person's services. Please don't. It is hard to get an insider to come into the process without any preconceived notions about what should happen and about whose opinion carries the most weight. An experienced facilitator can assure that all voices get heard, that the process moves according to schedule, and that any disagreement is handled correctly.

Using a Consultant

There are many consultants who do strategic planning. You can start by asking at your local AFP chapter, your association of nonprofits, or by asking other nonprofits in your community who they've used and whether they were happy with the person's abilities.

When talking to consultants, ask how many planning sessions they've done, whether they will produce the actual planning document, or just facilitate the retreat. You can probably save some money if you construct the actual plan and just use the facilitator for the retreat.

Be sure to ask if the consultant has experience with nonprofits. We've seen many plans developed for nonprofits, but done by consultants from the corporate planning world, and they often miss key issues such as governance and fundraising because these are not part of the corporate world.

Can You Find a Volunteer?

Often you can. Again, be sure this person has experience with the nonprofit sector. You might be able to get someone from another nonprofit to volunteer in exchange for someone from your organization helping it with its plan.

Or perhaps a board member who works for a large corporation will be able to enlist the services of the company's planning department, But again, see if they've ever done a nonprofit plan before engaging then.

To Recap

◆ Choose an interesting and fun location for your retreat—not your own meeting room.

◆ Have your planning cabinet determine who should be included in which parts of the retreat.

◆ Use an outside facilitator to ensure objectivity and an ability to keep the group on track.

Chapter Six

Values, Mission, and Vision

IN THIS CHAPTER

···➔ Clarifying values and beliefs

···➔ Review your mission

···➔ Establish a common vision for the future

The words perplex many nonprofit leaders: *What's the difference between mission and vision—between vision and values? Do we need them all? How do we use them? How do they drive our planning? How long should they be? Who develops them?* Quick answer—they should be developed collaboratively because their purpose is to reflect the entire organization. *How often do we need to revisit them, or change them?* All of these questions will be addressed in this chapter.

Values

Let's look at the importance of values and how they fit into strategic planning. Quite simply, values represent who you are as an organization. Your values as part of the culture of your organization help define what is right and wrong as well as the behaviors and perspectives that are important within your organization. Community members can look at these values or value statements to find out more about you and your organization.

Do you have a set of core values or a values statement already in place? If so, you have a head start in your planning and a framework that can help drive the direction as well as the content of your planning. As part of your strategic planning process, take the time to review those values, evaluate whether they are as relevant now as they were when you first developed them, and determine the need for clarification or change.

In our experience, many organizations may intuitively subscribe to a set of values but these values or a values statement have yet to be formally developed, written down, and distributed to stakeholders. If you haven't yet clarified the values of your organization, you can take advantage of the strategic planning process to develop your own values statement or a list of core values.

Some values might include:

◆ Learning

◆ Creativity

◆ Community

◆ Openness

◆ Caring

◆ Integrity

◆ Synergy

◆ Joy

◆ Diversity

The Northwest Vista College community created this list of values during their organizing years. Recently, these values have been renamed touchstones and they reflect the college's commitment to making a difference through learning and through service.

Example

So, how can you uncover your organization's values? These questions can help.

◆ What values are so vital to us that we would be willing to lose otherwise good talent if the people involved were not shining examples of this value?

◆ What values would you continue to bring to your work with this organization whether they were rewarded or not?

◆ Think of two or three people who you believe exemplify what this organization is all about. Now make a written list of all the things these people seem to have in common. What does this tell you about their values? Now look at three people who were a complete mismatch for the organization and ask how their apparent values were different from your first three "stars."

While these questions create a starting point, we think once you get into this process, you'll come up with an initial list which will most likely be very long. As you're making your list, consider the values of clients, customers, shareholders, employees, and the community.

So, what is the right number of values? Probably most people won't remember more than three, but we have often seen lists of ten or more. Having five is a good target although it may take some time and work to get there.

The Mission

So, you've reached consensus on the values and philosophy which guide your organization. What's next? As part of your strategic planning process, you'll want to clarify thinking about the mission. Does your mission statement say what you think it should say? Does it describe in a precise way the purpose of your organization?

Clarifying your mission statement may be as easy as saying yes, the mission statement adequately describes the overall purpose of the organization. On the other hand, you may decide to integrate new elements or delete elements which no longer apply.

To help identify which elements should be included in your mission statement, we have provided some questions to consider.

◆ Why does your organization exist?

◆ Who does the organization serve? Who should it serve?

Here is an example of values from a free medical clinic.

Values:

◆ **T**eamwork

◆ **R**espect

◆ **U**rgency

◆ **S**ervice

◆ **T**ransparency

Example

◆ What are the organization's most important programs and services?

◆ What makes the organization unique?

◆ What does the organization do best? What does it do least well?

◆ What is the organization most noted for in the community?

◆ What would the community lose if the organization were to cease to exist?

When you choose to modify the mission statement or to develop a new one, you should use the method that works best for your organizational culture. We've worked with organizations that have used a highly analytical and rational approach as well as those who favor highly creative and divergent methods. These approaches include everything from focused discussions to sharing stories and daydreams.

Your mission statement should be a specific, succinct articulation of what stakeholders wish your organization to be. Keep in mind that while the mission statement defines what your organization is, this statement also establishes limits or sets the parameters for your activities.

Helpful references for reviewing and developing the mission statement include the organization's articles of incorporation (there is always a statement of purpose in the articles, although this has generally been written by an attorney so you won't want to use it verbatim), charter, enabling legislation if applicable, board minutes, and annual reports. The mission statement establishes the guiding principles from which the strategic planning process flows. Your mission statement is truly unique to your organization.

What about wording of the mission statement? To get started, you may want to ask someone in the organization to do an online search of other nonprofits' mission statements. Then, engage participants in developing a list of key words and phrases relevant to the organization's products, services, markets, values, concern for public image, and, perhaps, priorities of activities for sustainability.

Once you have this list and the sampling of other mission statements from your online research, select a good writer to develop two or three statements using the key words and phrases as well as the research. To make the final selection, ask participants to vote for their preference of the

---

When You Know You Have Your Values Right

Just as we suggested questions to help you identify your core values, we also have a few questions or situations which will help you know when you have them right.

◆ You can ask newly hired staff members to describe what they see as the core value(s) of your organization and they describe the list, in their own words, without being trained.

◆ People may have lost their jobs over issues related to values.

◆ People who get promoted exemplify the stated values.

◆ People who live these values seek you out and want to work or volunteer with you.

observation

Some examples of good mission statements include:

◆ Make-A-Wish Foundation: We serve a unique and vital role in helping to strengthen and empower children battling life-threatening medical conditions.

◆ Charity Water: We're a nonprofit organization bringing clean, safe drinking water to people in developing countries.

◆ The LIVESTRONG Foundation: We unite, inspire, and empower people affected by cancer.

Example

An organization providing food and basic services for those in need decided they needed to update their mission statement. The board president appointed a task force of four people for the task. Over two months, the group met in person and communicated online about ideas. Several versions of a new mission statement were suggested and consensus was reached on the top three. Board members voted on the three finalists for the new mission statement and selected the winner.

Example

options presented by the writer. The statement garnering the most votes should become your mission. You might even find that the final "winner" is a hybrid of these phrases.

Vision for the Future

Where would your organization like to be in the future? The vision statement for your organization expresses that view and works in tandem with the mission. Frequently, the sentiments of the vision may seem lofty; the purpose of the vision, after all, is to inspire both the community and the clients. The vision builds on the ideas of the mission but expresses those ideas in abstract and futuristic terms.

While you may not clarify or review your mission, vision, and values in the order that we have presented them, the discussion of each should be a critical part of your strategic planning process. Earlier, we focused on examining the values and mission. The third component related to the overall purpose of your organization is your vision for the future.

What exactly is the vision? Simply stated, the vision describes your organization's preferred future state or what the organization wants to be in the future. Many ideas contribute to the vision but we have found that a vision springs from deeply held values, experiences, views of the future, intuition, and dreaming. You will want your vision to focus not just on how you see your organization in the future, but on what your vision is for your *community* in the future.

Developing a common vision can be one of the most enjoyable parts of your planning; however, you'll want to monitor how much time you spend on this part. Developing your vision for the future is an exercise in which time can quite easily get away from you.

Some of the most compelling vision statements answer the question "what would a perfect world look like?" Another good question to consider is "what would a world that no longer needed our organization look like?" Your thinking should also include ideas about the impact of your organization on the community in the future. What difference do you want to make?

Examples of good vision statements:

◆ Feeding America: A hunger-free America.

◆ Oceana: We seek to make our oceans as rich, healthy, and abundant as they once were.

◆ San Diego Zoo: To become a world leader at connecting people to wildlife and conservation.

Example

Key stakeholders should agree upon a realistic, credible, and attractive future for your organization. Together, you should seek to reach consensus on a destination toward which your organization should aim. Your vision should inspire enthusiasm, encourage commitment, be well-articulated, and easily understood. And, above all, your vision should be ambitious.

Answering the additional questions below will help you further identify the components of your organization's vision.

◆ What will the future business of the organization be?

◆ How large will the organization be?

◆ What programs will be conducted by the organization?

◆ What staff will be required? What volunteers will be required?

◆ What will the funding mix of the organization be?

◆ What facilities will the organization have?

◆ How will success be measured?

In addition to the vision for your organization, a good vision statement focuses on the vision you have for your community. Some questions you might ask to address this issue could include:

◆ What are the ultimate goals we are trying to achieve (i.e., end hunger, cure a disease, have a well-educated population, save a river)?

◆ What do we want our community to look like (i.e., free from violence, creative, strong work force)?

Other components you may wish to consider for your vision include board composition and structure as well as internal management structure and staffing requirements. What will your board look like in five, ten, fifteen, or more years? Will you need additional staff? As you look at each of these components, you can create and craft a vision for the future which will reflect your values and philosophy and provide a framework for clarifying your mission.

To Recap

◆ Your values provide a fundamental framework for planning and an important reference for critical decision making.

◆ A mission statement reflects your organizational values and philosophies and its wording can be both a motivational force and a guide through the strategic planning process and future decisions.

◆ With a common vision, your organization can transform ideas which begin with the mission into a futuristic view of where you are going.

Chapter Seven

Goals and Objectives

IN THIS CHAPTER

◆ What issues will you address?

◆ What are realistic and technically achievable goals?

◆ Board role in goal-setting

Many leaders are also perplexed about the difference between goals and objectives, wondering: *Is there a difference? How long a time period should our plan cover? How many goals can we reasonably expect to achieve in this timeframe? How many objectives do we need for each goal?*

We've found in helping groups work through the goals and objective phase, that this is one of the most difficult concepts for people to grasp. Many people, when hearing the word, "goal," think—*okay my goal needs to be specific—I need to lose fifty pounds.* Wrong thinking. Goals are really the broad-brushed result of achieving your objectives. A more accurate goal for the overweight person might be—to be healthy, to look good, or to have more energy. Each of those goals could have as an objective to lose fifty pounds.

Instead of starting with the objectives, though, think through the goals you should set for your plan.

Goals

Goals will help set the framework of your entire plan. Goals are the end result of where you want your organization to be. Some examples of goals might be:

◆ To create more awareness of our programs in the community

◆ To build a strong board that fulfills its governance role

◆ To develop an endowment fund that will assure our future in times of economic downturns

As you can see, none of these are measurable—they need the objectives that will undergird the goals.

To determine goals for your plan, look at your current situation; what would you like to improve?

Perhaps your board is not large enough, not connected in the community. Perhaps you are the best kept secret in town. There might be another organization providing similar programs that seems to get all the media attention and all the donations. Your goals are the targets to strive for. When you pick up a quiver full of arrows, you know there is a target that you want to hit. The objectives might be the circles within that target and when you reach the objective, you've hit the bull's eye. In the next chapter we'll talk more about the arrows in your quiver—the action steps you will take to reach the objective—the bull's eye.

For now, back to goals. Who establishes the goals, how many should you have, what to do when the goal is no longer relevant? These are some of the questions on which you will focus as you develop goals.

Who Establishes Goals?

Your board and executive leadership need to agree on goals. This is why the planning process, and who is involved in it, are so critical. Board members cannot simply say to staff—"okay folks, no one in the community knows about us—go change that." Or staff members cannot say to the board, "We need you to get involved in fundraising so our goal this year is to get every board member to give, get, or get off."

Goals set by either of these methods are doomed to failure. Groups usually work through the goal setting process at a strategic planning retreat (see **Chapter Five**). When you use the results of your internal and external analysis, your goals typically become fairly evident as the group brainstorms and talks about issues the organization is facing.

> Board and staff need to establish goals as a joint process.
>
> **!**
> important

How Many Goals?

Because goals are so broad, and each goal will need several objectives to support it, you shouldn't attempt to accomplish too many goals in one planning period. Three to five is generally a good number. You might, at your planning session, come up with seven or eight, even more in some cases. But to attempt to tackle that many goals at one time is usually impossible and everyone gets frustrated when the plan has set impossible objectives to reach.

A facilitator will help you through prioritizing goals. There are a number of ways to do this—open discussion, voting by listing possible goals, and having each participant put a sticky note or dot on the goals they think are most important, considering the timeline to accomplish the goals and defer longer-term goals to the next planning period, and considering your budget and resources needed to accomplish these goals.

For example, if you have a possible goal of becoming the largest organization of your type in the community—how far are you from that goal now, what will it take to get there (must you double in size or grow by ten-fold?) Do you have the money to invest in growth? Is it really important to be the largest, or is being the best at a specific program more important?

Some focused dialogue at your planning session should help you prioritize your goals and focus on the ones that everyone is excited about and believes doable.

> Lynne worked with an organization as it identified and prioritized goals. The process started with everyone taking a turn around the table and suggesting a goal. Individuals were allowed to "pass." When three people in a row "passed," the process stopped. The goals were listed on big white sheets of paper and taped to the wall. Then each participant received three purple dots and was asked to place their dots next to the top goals they wished to accomplish. The goals with the most dots were then placed on a list for additional discussion.
>
> **Example**

Objectives

For the practical, "just-do-it" people, this is the fun part of the planning process: determining objectives that are measurable and action-oriented.

So let's go back to those goals we talked about earlier and work on developing some objectives to support the goals:

Goal: Create more awareness of our programs in the community.

Objectives:

◆ Develop an interactive, up-to-date website by July 2015.

◆ Conduct a series of cultivation events for business leaders by December 2015.

◆ Develop a speaker's bureau, members of which will conduct at least one presentation per month for civic and professional clubs.

Goal: Build a strong board that fulfills its governance role.

Objectives:

◆ Engage a consultant to evaluate our current board structure and makeup by March 2015.

◆ Appoint a governance committee to develop board position descriptions and policies by June 2015.

◆ Identify at least three new board members each year who meet the criteria identified by the governance committee.

Goal: Develop an endowment fund that will assure our future in times of economic downturns.

Objectives:

◆ Appoint a planned giving subcommittee of the development committee by September 2015.

◆ Develop a list of potential planned giving prospects by December 2015.

◆ Launch a planned/major giving program in January 2016.

So, you can see that the objectives we've developed meet the SMART criteria discussed above. They contain very specific times to be done, are action oriented—develop, appoint, identify, etc.). They are realistic and time-defined. And, each objective can be measured to see how well you're performing in attaining your goals.

To Recap

◆ Goals are broad based and should be developed by board and staff together.

◆ Goals will become apparent during the planning process as you identify areas of weakness and opportunities for improvement.

◆ Objectives must be SMART—specific, measurable, action-oriented, realistic, and time-defined.

Objectives must be **SMART**:

◆ **S**pecific

◆ **M**easurable

◆ **A**ction-oriented

◆ **R**ealistic

◆ **T**ime-defined

definition

Chapter Eight

Strategies and Tactics (Action Steps)

IN THIS CHAPTER

- ┈┈➤ What is the process to develop strategies and activities to achieve your objectives?

- ┈┈➤ Who develops initial strategies?

- ┈┈➤ Who is responsible for making sure the action steps get done?

Once you outline your goals and objectives, you need strategies for implementing these objectives that will help you achieve your goals. Who is responsible for developing and approving strategies? Who implements them? What is the role of the board?

First, let's talk about the differences between strategies and tactics. One of the things some people don't like about strategic planning is that many of the references used have a lot of military correlation. The military plans campaigns, develops strategies, uses tactics to accomplish its end goal of winning the war. But, in the meantime, the strategies help win the little battles along the way. This is how it works in strategic planning as well.

If you don't like the military references, think of it as a chess game—the end result of which is to capture the opponent's chess pieces. But each move along the way is a tactic, which requires a lot of careful, thought-out strategy.

Developing Strategies

Let's go back to one of those objectives we talked about in **Chapter Seven**. And then, let's develop strategies that might help us achieve those objectives.

Remember that our overall goal was to increase awareness of your organization in the community.

Objectives:

- ◆ Develop an interactive, up-to-date website by July 2015.

◆ Conduct a series of cultivation events for business leaders by December 2015.

◆ Develop a speaker's bureau, members of which will conduct at least one presentation per month for civic and professional clubs.

Okay, so our first objective is to improve our website. What are some of the strategies we might use to achieve this?

Strategies:

◆ Review the websites of competitors and other agencies to see what we might want to incorporate in our website (and what we don't want).

◆ Engage a professional website designer.

◆ Ask our stakeholders for input on what should be in our website.

Each of these strategies answers the question of how will we go about improving our current website.

The second objective was to conduct a series of cultivation events for business leaders by December 2015. Some strategies we might employ to accomplish this objective include:

◆ Involve our board in developing a list of business contacts they have.

◆ Develop an economic impact statement that will impress business leaders on our case for support from the business community.

You get the idea. Strategies are the "how we will do this" step. To state the obvious, strategies put the *strategic* in strategic planning. Without them, your plan is not a strategic plan.

Tactics (or Action Steps)

Now, comes the tricky part. Most plans don't get implemented for one big reason—the failure to develop tactics, or action steps, to follow each objective and strategy.

Actions steps answer the three big questions:

◆ Who is going to do this?

◆ How much is it going to cost? (and/or how much is it going to bring in, if it is a revenue-generating activity)

◆ When is it going to get done?

This is the level of the plan we often call the tactical plan, the action plan, or the departmental plan. At this level, often the board and other stakeholders step out of the process unless the action steps are things they are responsible for implementing. Mid-level managers and other departmental staff take more responsibility for this step in the plan. A good strategic plan will have action plans for each functional area of the organization—a development plan, a program plan, a facility plan, a human resources plan, a financial plan.

Let's go back to one of the objectives we talked about and develop some action steps for that objective. The objective was to conduct a series of cultivation events for business leaders by December 2015. One strategy we developed was to involve our board in developing a list of business contacts they could invite to a cultivation event. Some resulting action steps based on this objective and strategy might include:

Action Step	Budget	Person/ Team Responsible	Time to Be Completed
Conduct a brainstorming session at the June board meeting to identify business leader contacts of board members	N/A	Executive Director/ Director of Development	June 2016
Ask board members to each host one cultivation event in 2017	N/A	Director of Development	September 2016
Secure facility and schedule events	N/A	Director of Development	October 2016
Plan agenda and prepare materials	$300	Development Committee/ Director of Development	December 2016
Send invitations to event	$200	Director of Development	January 2017 and monthly thereafter
Hold events	$6,000	Board, Executive Director, Development Committee, Director of Development	January 2017 and monthly thereafter

As you can see, the action steps clearly spell out who is going to do each item, when the item will be done, and how much it will cost.

If you take the plan to this level of detail, we guarantee it won't sit on a shelf gathering dust (or, more likely, sitting idle on your computer's drive), at least not if you follow our implementation and monitoring steps in the following chapters.

To Recap

◆ Objectives need to have strategies and actions steps in order to ensure they get done.

◆ Strategies answer the question, "how are we going to do this?"

◆ Action steps answer the questions, "when is this going to be done?" "how much will it cost (and/or generate)?" and "who is going to do it?"

Chapter Nine

Timelines, Budgets, and Areas of Responsibility

IN THIS CHAPTER

    ···→ What are the key tasks and fiscal and human resources required?

    ···→ What is a reasonable timetable?

    ···→ What are the roles of staff and the planning cabinet?

Give yourself a pat on the back—you have taken a monumental step forward in completing the planning process and documenting your vision for the future. You and your stakeholders have collectively put down in writing the results for which you and your organization will hold yourself accountable and the actions you will take to get there.

The next step, one in which many organizations stumble, is implementation. Our goal is to help you keep moving ahead and avoid "rocks in the road" or any stumbles. Keep on reading and you'll find advice, tips, and strategies to help you watch out for "rocks," continue the progress you've made so far, and ensure that you and your nonprofit achieve impact year after year.

Your planning team can help you sidestep those "rocks in the road" by breaking down strategies and action plans into manageable pieces, assigning specific responsibility for specific items to an individual or team, setting timelines, and establishing budgets for each strategy. In this chapter we will talk about implementation by answering these questions—who is going to do it, when is it going to be done, and how much will it cost (or raise?).

In **Chapter Eight**, we looked at how goals and objectives were translated into strategies. We began developing action steps or tactics for each objective. It's important to look at our tactics or action steps as a whole to ensure that the scope, length, and required effort to implement are, at the very least, realistic and sequenced appropriately. If you think about strategic planning as a journey, your tactical plan will be the road map or GPS that takes you to your destination.

In almost every organization that achieves success in implementing a strategic plan, we see two common threads. Implementation seems to run more smoothly when a nonprofit has what can best be described as a "change" mindset and when they use practical step-by-step approaches to translate strategies, goals, and objectives into very tangible actions.

And, these organizations continue to monitor progress on their actions, altering the direction or course of their journey when the environment in which they operate changes in some way.

When you take the time to help everyone understand the big picture and to see how their roles and work connect to those of others, you will be making a huge contribution towards the success and progress of the implementation of your strategic plan. You and your team will find that it makes sense for some action plans and changes to start before others.

One of the most significant aspects of implementation is the overall coordination and integration of your tactical plans. Careful planning enables you to outline the route to achieving the impact you envision and set the stage for progress to come.

For each objective and strategy, you will take a close look at detailed, specific action steps that will get you where you want to be. And, in this stage of the planning, you will review all your action steps and integrate them into an overall tactical plan. In this part of the process, you will examine and note key tasks, fiscal needs, and human resources required.

And, remember metrics and measurements. What metrics will you use to help measure progress along the way as well as the metrics that will measure your success? For each action step, you will want to define or at least have a pretty good idea about the following elements:

- *Results.* How will "success" be measured?

- *Action step leader.* Who will be responsible and involved in the work?

- *Key activities.* What steps need to be taken to achieve success?

- *Resources needed.* What equipment, funds, time, and people will be needed?

- *Links.* How will the action step impact other functions or areas of the organization? How will it affect other action steps?

- *Milestones.* What are the major events, accomplishments, or key decision points anticipated? How will you know whether your action step is on track?

- *Performance metrics.* What will you measure to gauge progress on your action step?

- *Timeline.* When will the action step begin and end?

And, we want to add here a note about outsourcing or using a consultant for implementation planning. Yes, the idea may be tempting, but for this stage, we agree that your staff, particularly senior managers, need to be deeply involved. They will have the most realistic sense of what you and your organization can accomplish over a certain time period. And, their buy-in to the deliverables and the timeline is essential.

Consultants may certainly be used as facilitators and help the implementation team stay focused on the task at hand, but at this part of the planning, we cannot overstate the importance of engaging your staff.

Timetable

After you've defined your action steps and outlined the elements of each, it's time to map your route and develop a timeline for reaching your destination and achieving the impact you envision. To do that, you'll need to consider how different tactics will affect each other or how they might be interdependent. And how will various action steps affect different parts of your organization.

Remember those "rocks in the road" we mentioned earlier? These rocks or bumps generally happen because most likely you have, through no fault of your own, placed competing demands on operations and other internal functions such as human resources, technology, and fundraising. You can easily avoid these bumps by proactively seeking to involve the heads of these departments early in the implementation of the plan.

And, while it's not a simple task, you can have a smoother journey by being alert to the need for making trade-offs. You'll see the need for these

> A faith-based organization providing basic needs services for needy individuals and families was renting warehouse and office space. Because of increasingly diversified needs, they worked with the building's owner to plan and construct modifications to the interior of the building. Then, the owner contacted them and said he had received an offer to buy the facility. So, the organization stopped work on the plans for modifications. And, to handle this "rock in the road," the board assigned the Building Committee a new task—locate another facility to either rent or purchase.
>
> **Example**

trade-offs as you determine which action steps must happen before others. When you recognize and make these trade-offs up front, you will have a much smoother road as you implement your strategic plan.

Truly, there is only so much work you and your staff can handle. And, some of your action steps will be exciting while other tactics may meet with some resistance. When you establish a plan to integrate your action steps, you keep the focus on your strategy rather than individual interests, advocacy, or other pressures.

By working together, you may find that it will be better for your organization to postpone or accelerate some action steps or perhaps add resources. When those involved in your various action steps, functional areas, and programs talk to each other, the result may lead to an enhanced sense of teamwork and help break up project and departmental silos.

Before you can establish a timeline for implementation, you need to have a clear overview of your action steps and an understanding of how your organization can most effectively integrate them. As you look at integrating action steps, consider these questions:

◆ Do you need to adjust any action step timelines because of interdependencies?

◆ Does one action step need to reach a milestone or finish before another can start or finish?

◆ Have you set realistic timelines considering your current workload?

◆ Do you have the funds available to complete the action step?

◆ If planned progress is made on each individual action step, is your organization on track to achieve the strategic priorities? Are any critical pieces missing?

You may want to create an integrated implementation timeline so that members of your management team can have an overview of how various action steps relate and depend on each other. This overview can also provide a concise picture of exactly what it is that your organization is undertaking.

Action Step Detail Chart

Objective	Action Step	Lead Person, Team	Timeline for Key Milestones	Resources Needed
	Step 1			
	Step 2			
	Step 3			
	Step 4			
	Step 5			

This chart enables you to integrate your action steps together over time, note key activities and milestones and keep track of interdependencies with other initiatives and other departments or functions.

This overview may also indicate that you have too many action steps and you most likely need to downsize the number of initiatives you plan to do. And, the overview may lead to some re-thinking on how to best sequence your action steps. Perhaps some steps you originally thought you would launch in the first year of your implementation may work best if pushed back into the second year.

> ### Action Step Timeline
>
> When you are developing your integrated picture of action steps with timelines and interdependencies, you may find it helpful to create a chart showing the action step, the objective to which it is linked, key activities and outcomes, lead person or team to which the action step is assigned, and a monthly or quarterly timeline in which you will indicate deadlines for key activities or milestones and interdependencies.
>
> **Example**

Making these kinds of adjustments is part of the normal implementation process. You'll probably discover that implementation may turn out to be a continuously evolving process, changing as you refine how you will travel towards your destination, deploy your strategies, and work towards achieving the impact you envision.

Roles of Staff and Planning Cabinet

At this level of planning, staff members will play a more active role, especially senior management. Middle level management and those in every functional area should also participate in developing tactical plans. These plans form the basis for linking the organization's strategic plan with long-term financial plans.

And, even more, successful implementation depends greatly on getting your staff on board with the strategy. Bringing the plan to life will probably require that staff members do things a little differently and helping them make those changes can be challenging.

So, are there any secrets to mobilizing your team for implementation? You will find that you can optimize your potential for success by focusing on two elements:

1.   Open communication related to the compelling case for the changes required.

2.   Alignment of individual staff members' performance goals to organizational strategic priorities.

Help your staff understand where they are headed and why as well as what they will need to do differently in the future. Especially useful are reminders to staff members of strategic priorities, the changes required to achieve them, and "wins" along the way as progress is made on action steps.

Staff participation in implementation can be particularly enhanced when individual performance goals are aligned with organization-wide and department-level goals. Your leadership team can help translate organization-wide goals into department-level goals with program directors of each department. The result will be a set of department-level goals which support the organization-wide goals.

Then, directors can work with those who report to them to develop individual performance plans which support department-level goals. In some organizations, individual performance goals may be primarily activity-based and not necessarily tied to organization-wide objectives. By creating this alignment, staff members will have specific, measurable goals directly linked with strategic priorities and these goals will be used in their annual performance reviews.

> One educational services organization used its strategic plan as the basis for development of specific action plans for staff departments and/or work groups. Each department developed an action plan related to one or more goals and strategies of the strategic plan. Each action item contained a one-year and three-year target and included a performance metric, person or area responsible, and start and end dates.
>
> **Example**

It's not always easy for staff members to see the connection between what they understand their jobs to be and their roles in implementation. If you have involved your staff in defining the action plans and creating the road map for the journey they will be taking, this task will be easier.

You may also find it helpful to encourage your staff to prioritize the activities in which they are engaged, elevate important strategic tasks, and de-prioritize others. Staff members then see implementation-related activities as their core responsibilities, rather than additional tasks on top of the work they are already doing.

> In that educational services organization mentioned above, staff members also used the work group action plans to then develop individual action plans which correlated and aligned with the work group or department action plans. Similar metrics were used to track progress on the individual action plans. And, supervisors used reports on progress made on individual action plans as one of the measurements in annual performance evaluations of each staff member.
>
> **Example**

Once you have translated strategic priorities to individual staff member objectives as part of performance reviews, you may also want to create incentives and rewards that will help everyone stay on track during the implementation of your plan and help overcome challenges as they arise.

And what about the planning cabinet? What role do they play during implementation?

You may choose to have the planning cabinet continue to meet after your strategic plan has been prepared and approved by the board. When this group continues to work after the approval of the strategic plan, its role shifts into one focused on monitoring progress on the plan.

This group works with staff to gauge progress and to help in moving the implementation process forward. You may also choose to appoint committees to provide support for the achievement of the various action plans of your organization. These committees can be formed to support staff members in their implementing role. If your nonprofit organization is too small to have an adequate number of staff members for implementation, you can use these action plan committees to assist the executive director in implementation.

To Recap

◆ Tactical plans should be coordinated and integrated to identify interdependencies on key tasks, fiscal needs, and human resources.

◆ An integrated implementation timeline will provide an overview of how various action steps relate and depend on each other.

◆ Open communication and alignment of individual performance goals with strategic priorities enhance your staff engagement in achieving the impact envisioned by your organization.

Chapter Ten

Financing the Plan

IN THIS CHAPTER

◆ What resources are needed and what are your budget projections?

◆ Will available financing mean adjustments in some programs and timetables?

◆ Do you have adequate and available staff and volunteers?

◆ What technology is needed to implement your plan?

You've outlined an integrated implementation plan for your tactics. But, how will you pay for it all? We will delve now into more details on budgeting and financing your carefully crafted plan. We will also look at the human and technology resources needed to implement your plan.

What are the fiscal resources you will need to complete your tactical plan? Taking the time to include fiscal planning as part of your tactical planning can help ensure effective use of resources and increase your chances for a return on your investment.

Your financial planning will look at these important issues:

◆ Future revenue stream(s) and mix

◆ How financial resources will be used to advance strategies

◆ Funding sources

◆ Timing of resources to be used

In the example of action steps to achieve the strategy of involving the board in developing a list of business contacts they could invite to a cultivation event in **Chapter Eight**, we included expenditures for materials for the event, invitations, and the actual event. We then incorporate these expenses into our annual budget.

Action Step	Budget	Person/ Team Responsible	Time to Be Completed
Conduct a brainstorming session at the June board meeting to identify business leader contacts of board members	N/A	Executive Director/ Director of Development	June 2016
Ask board members to each host one cultivation event in 2017	N/A	Director of Development	September 2016
Secure facility and schedule events	N/A	Director of Development	October 2016
Plan agenda and prepare materials	$300	Development Committee/ Director of Development	December 2016
Send invitations to event	$200	Director of Development	January 2017 and monthly thereafter
Hold events	$6,000	Board, Executive Director, Development Committee, Director of Development	January 2017 and monthly thereafter

Thus, the budget for 2016 will include $300 and the 2017 budget will include $6,200 for these action steps.

If our objective is to expand services to a specific audience and our strategy requires a new building, that expense would be incorporated in the capital budget.

Just as we look at the fiscal resources needed to implement our tactical plan, we will also look at the human resources required. Can we complete our tactical plan with existing staff and board members? And, who will be responsible for each tactic? A good rule of thumb is that you should assign responsibility to the highest level person below the CEO. And, assign only one or two people—any more than two and no one is responsible (or at least it seems that way).

Resources

Each action step you undertake needs adequate resources over time. And that necessity underscores how important it is to develop a resource plan for action steps. By creating an overview of resource planning for action steps, you can help your staff think in a very practical way about the costs associated with implementing a specific tactic.

The overview on resource planning should include capital expenditures, start-up costs, ongoing costs, and estimated savings.

For our purposes, capital expenditures are fixed assets that depreciate over time. Start-up costs are one-time or time-limited costs related to the beginning of an action step such as hiring a consultant. Ongoing costs are those that continue over the course of completing the action step. An example of ongoing costs is staff costs. These costs will occur annually after the beginning date.

Estimated savings include any savings that might be accrued through increased revenue such as higher

Capital and Ongoing Expenses

Capital expenditures: These include acquiring, repairing, or upgrading a physical asset such as land, a building, or equipment. The asset must have an expected useful life of more than one year, according to the AFP Fundraising Dictionary.

Ongoing expenses: These costs include staff costs, phone and internet services and other items related to day-to-day operations of the organization.

Example

ticket sales or reduced costs such as fewer staff. These savings may include one-time or ongoing savings. This planning overview makes it easier to estimate the true cost of each initiative by listing dollars and cents for each of the four budget categories.

Many tactics require different parts of your nonprofit to work together, so they may not be owned by one single department or have a champion during the budgeting process when the tough decisions and trade-offs are made. Caution: when you make detailed departmental budget decisions without considering the resources required for these activities, you may risk underfunding them.

One way you can prevent underfunding is to begin the annual budgeting process with a focus on tactics and strategic priorities. Managers can allow time to adjust across several versions and scenarios. Such strategically-focused budgeting, though, requires tough conversations about what you can and must do to achieve your most important goals. And then, everyone must be committed to following through with the necessary resources.

Making Adjustments

Implementing action steps may likely require shifting finances or even acquiring new resources to support strategic goals. Will you have to change programs or timetables to ensure adequate financing?

For an organization with only a small amount of unrestricted financial support, the process of aligning resources to action steps may require aggressive fundraising to support strategic priorities so funding restrictions don't slow down progress.

However, you may find that a new strategic focus will position you to raise funds more successfully. For example, perhaps one of your goals was to become less dependent on grant funding and one of the resulting objectives was to develop an individual giving strategy. This new strategy, in the short run, might have costs associated with it such as engaging a consultant, conducting those donor cultivation activities, etc. But, in the long run, this strategy should put your organization in a much stronger financial position as major gifts start coming in as a result of your strategies.

> ### A Strategy and a Budget
>
> One organization established accurate and up-to-date donor and prospect records as a priority. The strategy they proposed to achieve that objective was to select a new constituent relations management software. They allocated $100,000 for the purchase and were able to raise the funds necessary to obtain the application they selected.
>
> **Example**

Your organization might face having to shift funds at the beginning of a new strategic emphasis or program, then see funds become more available once the strategy and related action steps are more fully developed. This positive impact results because you now have a clear action plan connected to the strategic plan and that in turn can provide a more compelling case for support to potential funders.

Staff and Volunteers

As part of the implementation process, your organization will need to determine whether or not you have an adequate number of staff and volunteers to accomplish your objectives and tactics and achieve the impact you envision. It's a tough question and there are no easy answers.

Finding the answer to that question is part of the open communication you will need to have with staff members as you make the implementation journey. Be proactive in soliciting staff concerns. Try to keep in mind that change isn't always comfortable for everyone and that fear of the unknown can sidetrack your progress and result in an unscheduled stop on one of those "rocks in the road."

Some organizations have developed a system to evaluate whether to keep, change, or stop individual programs. Staffing and volunteer levels are key considerations in this evaluation. The implementation process almost always requires adjustments because of changing conditions such as the economy and gaps in readiness.

Does your organization rely on volunteers? If so, do you have an adequate number of volunteers to tackle the tasks included in your action steps? Many organizations such as Habitat for Humanity depend a great deal on volunteers to help provide the human resources for their critical programs and services.

As part of your implementation planning, your organization should review the volunteer program and its participants to determine whether the number of those helping now will be adequate for your upcoming tasks and action steps. Will you need volunteers with different skills? How long do volunteers typically remain active with

---

Checklist for Aligning Financial Resources

Consider these questions when making important decisions on financial resources:

❑ Looking at your strategic goals, what programs should be continued, changed in some way, or dropped?

❑ Are key tactics getting the resources necessary for success?

❑ Does your overall budget reflect your strategic priorities in terms of spending across objectives and tactics and across the organization as a whole?

❑ If you are anticipating a tighter budget in the year ahead than the one in which the plan was crafted, what principles will your management team use to make the tough calls?

Example

---

your nonprofit? How will fluctuations in the number of volunteers impact the services in which they are involved?

What you may find helpful as you move forward and strive to keep your every-day decisions consistent with long-term strategic priorities is to bring significant issues to the board on a quarterly basis. This action can help an organization balance big-picture goals with day-to-day work.

Technology

You have developed an overview of action steps you are taking to improve the program and services of your nonprofit. Good job. As part of your strategic plan and obtaining the resources to achieve the impact you envision, you are investing in the future. Have you overlooked anything? What about technology? Have you included technology as part of your planning and part of that investment? Will technology increase your return on investment?

Realistically, your organization is not going to implement anything that does not improve some aspect of your operations, programs, or

---

An arts organization developed a series of outdoor performances in city parks to expand its outreach and to help develop and expand its audience. Each program featured a well-known regional music or dance performer and the opportunity for families to enjoy the performances on blankets and lawn chairs under the stars. With marketing and advertising costs, the logistical costs for vendors to sell food and drinks, and volunteers as well as contract workers needed to help stage each production, the organization realized after one season that the outdoor performances simply cost too much and did not provide enough return on investment to warrant continuing them for another season, even though the performances had attracted a small, loyal following.

Example

services. To determine whether technology and/or an investment in technology can enhance the effectiveness of your implementation process and subsequent results, you will want to take a close look at how you can most effectively and efficiently provide your programs and services.

Are you really providing optimal services to your constituencies if you are not using the most appropriate tools and technology to provide those services? When you determine that technology or enhancements to technology can help you improve services and accomplish your action steps according to the timeline you've developed, you can make technology and technology planning a part of the implementation process.

> An educational organization needed to expand internal and external communications to achieve marketing objectives. The current email system was inadequate for the various audiences they served and the diverse messages they sent. So, they surveyed an array of options and determined that a subscription to an email marketing service would best address their communication needs. They added the cost for the service as a line item in their annual budget.
>
> **Example**

To Recap

◆ Create a resource plan to outline resources and budget necessary for implementation of your strategic plan.

◆ Evaluate financing availability and determine criteria for adjusting programming and timetables.

◆ Communicate openly about staff and volunteer needs related to implementation and the timetable.

◆ Make technology planning a part of your implementation.

Chapter Eleven

The Product

IN THIS CHAPTER

---→ Who will write the plan?

---→ What are the components of the plan?

---→ What will the plan look like?

Remember, planning is both a process and a product. Both are equally important. We've talked about the process; now let's turn to the product. Who writes the plan? What does it look like? In this chapter we will include sample plan segments and templates so you can develop a plan that works for your organization.

During the planning process, you have most likely discovered that some of the participants are very process-oriented people. They love doing the research, building consensus, analyzing past results. But be careful that you don't get so wrapped up in the process that your forget about the end result—the product itself.

We've seen planning products—the plan—that range from a one-page graphic illustration of the plan to a fifty-plus page document. The size of the document isn't as important as the answer to the big question—will this plan work for us, will it be a living, breathing, implementable plan, or will it sit on the shelf gathering dust until it's time to be updated?

Sample Plan Components

We thought we would give you some sample plan components so you can see what we mean. With these in hand, you can choose the right style plan for your organization.

Sample SWOT Analysis

Here is a SWOT Analysis one group used. This summary is the result of a brainstorming session done at a board/staff retreat.

2015-2018 SWOT MATRIX

Strengths	Weaknesses
Current resources/capabilities Maintain/build/grow/leverage	Current deficiencies Remedy/improve/overcome
◆ Staff	◆ Marketing/PR Capabilities
◆ Comprehensive Programs	◆ Public Awareness
◆ Facilities	◆ Volunteer Recruitment
◆ Low Debt	◆ Budgeting
◆ Efficient/Low Cost Delivery	◆ Identifying Funding Needs
◆ Reputation	◆ BOD Leadership
◆ Meet a Critical Community Need	◆ IT Capabilities
◆ Something for Everyone in Recovery	◆ Statistics/Tracking
◆ Proactive	◆ Alumni Program
◆ Passion	
◆ Commitment	
◆ Large Referral Base	

Opportunities	Threats
Future favorable factors Prioritize/pursue	Future unfavorable factors Minimize/eliminate
◆ Volunteer Recruitment	◆ Political Climate
◆ Marketing	◆ Economy
◆ Public Relations	◆ Diminishing Public Funding
◆ Community Education	◆ Funding Mix
◆ Web Site Development	
◆ Staff Expansion & Development	
◆ Women's Housing & Programs	
◆ BOD Leadership Development	
◆ Collaboration w/ other Agencies	
◆ Revenue Generating Activities	
◆ Fundraising	
◆ Community Corrections Center	

Here is a chart you can use to develop your strengths, weaknesses, opportunities, and threats:

Strengths	Weaknesses

Opportunities	Threats

Sample Goals and Objectives

Although every organization's goals will be unique to the organization, these sample goals and objectives give you a good idea how to ensure that goals are broad-based and objectives are SMART (specific, measurable, action-oriented, realistic, and time-defined)

Goals and Objectives

Overarching Goal: To create a sustainable organization

Goals & Objectives:

I. Develop a strong governance structure

    a. Develop governance/committee structure by October 2015

    b. Expand the board to thirteen individuals by December 2016

    c. Provide ongoing board education beginning January 2017

II. Develop strong programs and events

    a. Develop a structure for member meetings by December 2015

    b. Develop an interactive website by December 2015

    c. Develop program plan by June 2016

III. Create meaningful ways to involve volunteers

    a. Develop volunteer opportunities by May 2016

    b. Develop volunteer position descriptions by August 2016

    c. Recruit volunteers by December 2016

IV. Increase fundraising activities to assure our future

    a. Develop a case for support by December 2015

    b. Develop a grants calendar by December 2016

    c. Develop a membership program by June 2016

    d. Plan and implement a successful fundraising event by June 2016

    e. Develop and implement a corporate appeal by January 2016

    f. Develop the infrastructure for fundraising by December 2015

    g. Investigate possibility of owning a building and develop funding for building if feasible by December 2017

Once your goals and objectives have been established you can use a working planning grid like the one shown here during your planning meetings to fill in dates, budgets, and persons responsible.

Exhibit A: Working Planning Grid

Goal	Objective	Strategy	Budget	Responsibility	Completion Date
Develop a more diversified funding stream/ less dependence on grants	Create a development plan by xx/xx/xx	Identify resources: books, samples of plans	N/A	Development Committee	
	Develop infrastructure by xx/xx/xx	Investigate if current software will work or if new software is needed			
		Develop gift acceptance policies			
		Review/develop procedures			
		Develop a case for support			
Improve Donor Relations	Develop a Moves Management Program by xx/xx/xx	Research potential funders			
		Develop priority funder list			
		Develop communication strategies for donors/prospects			
		Develop donor/ prospect contact forms			
Increase Volunteer Involvement in Fundraising	Increase board involvement in fundraising by xx/xx/xx	Identify areas in which SFYS can involve volunteers			
		Identify communities from which to find volunteers			
		Develop volunteer position descriptions and policies			

Goal	Objective	Strategy	Budget	Responsibility	Completion Date
		Invite board members to work their spheres of influence			
		Establish board expectancies for fundraising			

See **Appendix D** for a template of the working planning grid.

Sample Grid for Goals and Objectives With Action Steps

Once the goals and objectives have been determined and your team assigns strategies and action steps to each objective, you can place all this information into a grid similar to the one shown here:

Exhibit B: Goals, Objectives and Tasks

Goals, Objectives, Task	Responsibility Of	Anticipated Expense	Start Date	End Date
Goal 2 Involve Board in Development Efforts				
Objective 2.1 Structure Board as a Fundraising Board				
Tasks 2.1.1 Develop Board Organizational Chart	Consultant			11/15/2016
2.1.2 Develop position descriptions for all Board members and committees	CEO/ Consultant	$250		12/15/2016
2.1.3 Recruit Board members	CEO/Board			1/15/2017
Objective 2.1 Anticipated Income/Expense		$250		
Objective 2.2 Establish Development Committee				
Tasks 2.2.1 Develop position description for Development Committee	Consultant	$250		12/15/2016
Task 2.2.2 Recruit chairperson for Development Committee	CEO/CDO/ Board			1/15/2017
Task 2.2.3 Recruit Development Committee members	CDO/DC Chair			3/15/2017
Task 2.2.4 Have Development Committee affirm plan and enlist Board's help to implement plan				
Objective 2.2 Anticipated Income/Expenses		$250		

See template in **Appendix D**.

Another way to structure this is using a database program to enumerate the goals, objectives, and action steps and arrange them into a document like this:

Exhibit C: Strategic Plan Goals and Objectives

Goal	Objective	Strategy	Budget	Responsibility	Timeline
Stabilize giving for 2016	Raise an additional $25,000 for Sports Luncheon	Review lists with Board members	N/A	CDO	10/18/2016
		Prepare materials for sponsorship appeal	N/A	CDO	10/20/2016
		Conduct sponsorship appeal	$25,000	Board	1/30/2017
	Raise $20,000 from foundations by December 31, 2016	Research foundations	N/A	CDO	12/31/2016
		Prepare proposals as needed			
	Raise $7,000 from direct response fundraising by December 31, 2016	Prepare year-end mailing	$3,000 ($TBD)	CDO	10/15/2016
		Conduct telephone follow-up	$2,000	Board	11/30/2016
		Promote Day of Giving in December through social media	$2,000	CDO	11/15/2016
Raise $177,000 by December 31, 2017	Raise $10,000 in major gifts by December 31, 2017	Review lists of prospects, add to lists	N/A	CDO/Board	12/15/ 2016
		Develop case for support	N/A	CDO	12/31/2016
		Conduct cultivation events	($1,000)	CDO/Board	1/1/2017– 6/30/2017
		Build Development Committee	N/A	CDO/CEO/ Development Committee Chair	1/31/2017

Goal	Objective	Strategy	Budget	Responsibility	Timeline
		Plan major gift approaches during 2017	$10,000	CDO/Board/ Development Committee	3/1/2017– 6/30/2017
	Raise $30,000 in local grants by December 31, 2017	Prepare list of foundations with trustees listed	N/A	CDO	1/31/2017
		Review list with Board	N/A	CDO	2/28/2017
		Prepare grant proposals	$ TBD	CDO	Ongoing starting 3/1/2017

See template in **Appendix D**.

Benchmarking

Once you have your goals and objectives outlined, the next critical step is to arrange the planning document so that you can easily benchmark success. One way to do this is to arrange all your goals and objectives by areas of responsibility, budget, and timeline. This will accomplish several things for you:

◆ The timeline allows the planning cabinet to monitor progress and ensure that tasks are on schedule.

◆ The budget allows the CFO and CEO to prepare and monitor the budget for implementing the plan

◆ The areas of responsibility can be given to each person or team responsible so they can track their own progress.

For an example of a benchmarking plan arranged by area of responsibility, see **Appendix C**. A template for a benchmarking plan is included in **Appendix D**.

In **Appendix B**, we have included a sample plan to help you determine what works best for your organization.

Who Will Prepare the Planning Document

Often if a consultant is engaged to assist with the plan, it will be this person's responsibility to draft the planning document for approval by the planning cabinet and all those involved in developing the plan. If a consultant is not used, the planning cabinet will need to assign this responsibility to one person. The cabinet should decide the format of the plan, however, to provide guidance to the person assembling the document.

You can "pretty up" the plan with graphics if you prefer that presentation style. Many groups opt for this style when the plan will be shared with funders or volunteers.

Some examples are in **Appendix B**.

To Recap

♦ The process and the product are both important.

♦ One person should be assigned to draft the planning documents for the approval of the planning cabinet.

♦ It will be critical for the plan to contain benchmarking tools in order to monitor progress against the plan.

Chapter Twelve

Ensuring Board Buy-In

IN THIS CHAPTER

- ◆ Presenting to the planning cabinet

- ◆ Plan represents details of earlier board input on goals

- ◆ Board adoption as a policy document

The board's role in planning is critical to its adoption. Board members should be intimate with the plan's goals and willing to accept responsibility for the things appropriate to the governance role of the board—assuring the board is operating efficiently and legally, recruitment of appropriate board members, oversight of the organization's finances. This chapter will discuss how to ensure that your board is on board with the plan.

Board members or at least a significant number of them should be involved in virtually every step of the planning process. And, thus, as each component piece of the plan comes together, one or more board members will be familiar with that piece.

Who Writes the Plan?

In the last chapter, we talked about the components of the plan and various ways the finished document might look. Generally, a member of the planning cabinet serves as plan writer. The person who has taken the most meticulous notes during planning meetings might be invited to prepare the first draft of the plan for review by the planning cabinet. This could be the consultant or facilitator.

Various subcommittees might assist the plan writer by gathering specific information on special sections of the plan. The plan writer assembles the decisions and input which has emerged from planning meetings as well as contributions from subcommittees into a cohesive document. Keep in mind, though, that the plan should be much more than simply a record of planning meetings.

Or, you may choose several people to write different sections of the document. Then, another group of people can edit the document after completion to ensure consistency and readability. Using this option,

```
┌─────────────────────────────────────────────┐
│          Elements of a Strategic Plan         │
│                                               │
│   ◆  Mission                                  │
│                                               │
│   ◆  Vision                                   │
│                                               │
│   ◆  Values/Guiding Principles                │
│                                               │
│   ◆  Strategic Direction                      │
│                                               │
│   ◆  Goals                                    │
│                                               │
│   ◆  Measures of Success (Strategic Metrics)  │
│                                               │
│   ◆  Strategies                               │
│                              ┌──────────────┐ │
│                              │ 🔍 finition  │ │
└──────────────────────────────└──────────────┘─┘
```

you will not place the burden of writing or editing on one person.

The document includes updated mission, vision, and values, as well as finalized strategic issues, goals, and strategies. A draft should be distributed to planning cabinet members for comments and feedback. At the next meeting, planners can exchange ideas, suggestions, and recommendations about the content and format of the planning document. This feedback can then be incorporated into the finalized document.

Board Input on Goals

In the design of the future of a nonprofit organization, members of the board of directors really serve as the primary architects. They have the lion's share of responsibility for the success of the nonprofit and must also provide the critical link between the nonprofit and the external environment in which the organization operates. In addition, the board must ensure that the nonprofit effectively addresses the needs of its constituents and reaches the community it intends to serve.

That's a lot to think and worry about. One of the best ways for board members to ease that worry is to join hands with the executive director to establish a strategic planning process, participate in that process, and approve the final strategic plan. It's that easy, or, you might say, that challenging.

Whatever your feelings about the process, we can tell you from our experience that the board should jump enthusiastically into the planning game, play a key role in every step of the planning process, and provide counsel and input on the finished product.

Here are three areas in which the board can be particularly helpful and effective:

◆ Gathering and analyzing information about the external environment, current political trends, or new financial opportunities

◆ Contributing to discussions related to current and proposed programs and services

◆ Helping to evaluate financial resource projects and set program priorities

When the board has been intimately involved in the entire planning process, they become "owners" of the plan. The process becomes a platform for them to debate new programs, evaluate existing programs, examine fund raising objectives, and review the organization's capabilities and strategies. The process provides an opportunity to look forward, determine what really matters, and recognize whether the organization needs to change.

Board members get input, discover and put into place planning themes, agree on priorities, and

> A social services agency asked board members to participate in the "Listening Project." As part of the strategic planning process, board members interviewed donors, clients, staff members at collaborating organizations and volunteers to gain input and feedback on their agency.
>
> **Example**

set measurable goals. When your board is actively involved in each of these facets of your planning, you have created a powerful process to help determine what will have the greatest impact in fulfilling the mission of your organization. You end up with a workable plan plus you gain a board whose members feel energized and engaged because they were involved in the development of the plan.

Adopting the Plan

The plan writing team and planning cabinet may consider several drafts of the plan before developing the final version of the plan which will be presented to the board of directors. In addition to the plan, the planning cabinet may develop a report outlining the planning process, internal and external assessments, and prioritized needs.

As a separate item on the agenda of a regular board meeting, the plan should be formally presented to the board for its consideration and adoption as a policy document. Ideally, board members will have read the plan before the board meeting, however, you may find it beneficial to have a planning cabinet representative provide a verbal overview of the contents of the plan.

A report on the planning process should include a description of the planning process and note who was involved. Mention the formation of a planning cabinet, members participating, and the roles and responsibilities of the cabinet. If you use a facilitator, you should name the facilitator and describe the role of the facilitator in your process.

Instead of a separate report, you may choose to include an executive summary as part of the final plan document. This section provides background and history on the organization as well as an overview of the direction and results of the strategic planning process. In this report or summary, the organization outlines the goals they have established and describes how the plan is organized.

Example

Once the board has formally adopted your plan, board members or a special task force or committee should also plan to check on the progress your organization is making in accomplishing the goals and objectives of the plan. The planning cabinet may fulfill this role if you choose. Checkpoints and reporting on the plan should occur at regular board meetings and may be scheduled every three months. The time for checking may vary based on the type of objective; you should regularly schedule monitoring and review of progress on the plan as a part of the board's business.

To Recap

◆ Your planning cabinet oversees writing and editing the plan.

◆ Board members gain "ownership" of the plan by active involvement in every step.

◆ The planning cabinet presents the plan to the board for formal adoption.

Chapter Thirteen

Implementing the Plan

IN THIS CHAPTER

···→ Develop annual work plans.

···→ Staff work plans can help in performance evaluations.

···→ Establish annual, detailed development plan.

The staff role is making sure the plan gets implemented and understanding the barriers that might prevent full implementation of the plan. This chapter will discuss the importance of developing departmental action plans to assure implementation of the full plan. In particular, we will address the development plan, which is needed to obtain the funding for the implementing your goals.

One of the biggest reasons plans do not get implemented—be they strategic plans, development plans, marketing plans, etc.—is that the planning body has not answered the "Big Three" questions referred to in **Chapter Eight**.

When putting together your plan, you need to address all three of these areas.

Responsibilities

Each department will develop its own action plan once the goals and objectives have been approved by the board and planning cabinet. The entire planning group does not need to get overly involved in the action steps (tasks) for each department; if you expect everyone to get that deeply involved, enthusiasm will wane very quickly and board members will feel they are micro-managing the organization instead of governing it.

The Big Three Questions

1. Who is going to do this task?

2. How much is this going to cost (or raise, if it is an income producing goal)?

3. When is it going to get done?

important

Be certain that each department is aware, going into the planning process, that it will be responsible for its own detailed plan.

The development plan is particularly important because the development office is often responsible for raising the additional money required to implement planning goals. For example, if your organization needs a new facility or major renovation, your development office will plan and implement a capital campaign to ensure the funds are available for this major undertaking. The board, of course, makes the ultimate decision to move forward with a major building project and should approve any capital campaign goal attached to this project, but it is not responsible for developing the tasks associated with a capital campaign.

Some areas of responsibility involving a major building campaign might include:

Task	Responsibility
Engage architect to do facility study	Board Facility Committee and CFO
Approve architectural plans	Board and ED
Approve capital campaign goal	Board
Research capital campaign consultants	CDO
Engage consultant	Board
Work with consultant to develop capital campaign plan	CDO
Work with consultant to develop campaign case statement	CDO

There should always be a person, persons, or committee responsible for each task in the plan. In most cases assigning a specific person is best so the planning cabinet can talk directly to the person involved. Putting names in the plan, however, can be tricky because people come and go. So the best option is to list areas of responsibility as executive director, development committee chair, or director of programs. Of course, as new people are brought into any of these positions they should be given the plan and especially the part of the plan that shows their specific responsibility (more about this in **Chapter Fourteen**).

Expenses/Income Budget for Plan

It will be critical to assign an anticipated cost or expected revenue for each item in the plan. Often plans do not get implemented because the planning group had great vision and enthusiasm, but perhaps was not realistic in its cost projections, or was overly optimistic about revenue generating activities. Once the plan tasks have been determined, you must attach costs and revenues to any items that will involve either or both of those items. Of course, some tasks do not affect the bottom line, and in this case you should put N/A (not applicable) in the budget line for these items, so your budget plan doesn't look as though you simply forgot to determine how one item will affect your bottom line. If you don't know the exact cost, at least estimate. Your financial officer needs to be part of this process because, if for no other reason, the CFO is often a good reality check.

> A social services agency agreed on an objective to move the services provided at a satellite location to its main facility. The services were provided in a building that was owned by the agency. Before the agency could move the services, they would need to find a buyer for the existing facility so that necessary upgrades to the agency's main campus could be made to accommodate the services. The agency was unable to find a buyer for the property, so the objective was postponed.

stories from the real world

An example of what a planning budget might include is the costs and revenue associated with running a special event:

Task	Projected Income	Projected Expense
Contract with facility for dinner		$100,000
Send invitations to dinner	$250,000	$10,000
Engage entertainment		$50,000
Secure gifts for silent auction	$300,000	$30,000
Purchase decorations		$30,000

Timelines

The last of three questions—when is it going to be completed—is another important milestone. There should be a start date and an end date to each task. Suppose, for example, your facilities committee has been assigned the task of engaging an architect to do a facility feasibility study to see if the organization needs to renovate or purchase a new facility. The committee will need some time to accomplish this task, so there should be action steps such as:

A museum decided that bringing in a major exhibition would accomplish two objectives: expanding its audience and increasing revenue. Costs involved in the action step of bringing the major exhibition to the museum proved too high and thus, for the short term, the museum opted to arrange for a series of smaller exhibitions targeting specific and different audiences and postpone the major exhibition.

Example

◆ List five architects we will consider for the job.

◆ Prepare a list of interview questions for the architects.

◆ Interview and select the architect to do the study.

◆ Study completed.

◆ Study presented to the board.

The timeline for this task should take into consideration how many people are on the committee, their schedules and available time, and the time it will take for the selected architect to complete the study. So the timetable might look something like this:

Task	Timeline
List five architects we will consider for the job	Start 6/1/16 Completed by 6/30/16
Prepare a list of interview questions for the architects	Start 6/1/16 Completed by 6/30/16
Interview and select the architect to do the study	Start 7/1/16 Complete by 7/31/16
Study completed	Start 8/1/16 Complete by 9/30/16
Study presented to the board	At 10/16/16 board meeting

Remember that a plan is similar to a budget, it is not written in stone. Although you should try to stick as closely as possible to your timelines, budgets, and areas of responsibility, things will happen that prevent this.

Your program director might leave and the position is open for two months while you hire a replacement. So what happens to the tasks assigned to this person? They either need to be reassigned or timelines adjusted. The event we mentioned above might end up not selling enough tickets, or the silent auction might bring in less than anticipated. (This is why you'll want a development plan with multiple funding streams so if one falls short, another can make up the difference). Or it might take longer to select an architect than the facility committee anticipated because one of its committee members got sick, one was swamped at work, and one resigned. So remember—"stuff" happens!

To Recap

◆ All planning tasks need to answer the "big three" questions: Who is going to do this task, how much will it cost (or raise), and when is it going to get done?

◆ Each department is responsible for developing its own action plan including the tasks that answer the big three questions.

◆ Remember that the plan is not written in stone.

Chapter Fourteen

Monitoring and Evaluating the Plan

IN THIS CHAPTER

◆ The planning cabinet periodically reviews effectiveness of activities.

◆ The cabinet reports on progress of the plan.

◆ The board should use the strategic plan as a basis for board meeting agendas.

Okay, the plan is done! Yes! But now, who holds everyone's feet to the fire? The planning cabinet is responsible for periodic evaluation and possible adjustment of the plan as the year progresses. Remember that the role of the cabinet is not to implement the entire plan, but to ensure implementation. Each individual department is responsible for getting things done internally, and the board and other volunteers will usually be involved in implementing other areas, especially those that relate to the external operations—creating awareness, donor relations, and the like.

All of this will be easier to accomplish if you build benchmarks into the plan from the beginning.

Remember the three big questions from the last chapter—who is going to do it, how much will it cost (or raise), and when is it going to be done. These three areas are all part of your benchmarking system.

Once all the plan's objectives have tasks assigned to them, you will list them as shown in **Chapter Eight**. The next step is to pull each of the three areas apart and list benchmarks for each person or team, all budget items, and an overall timeline.

So, your benchmarks will look like the ones show here.

Responsibility Benchmarks

Here is a sample of what the responsibilities for the board might look like:

Goal	Objective	Strategy	Action Steps	Responsibility	Budget	Timeline
Create community awareness	Develop and implement marketing plan	Utilize professional resources that may be available both pro bono and paid	Approve plan	Board	$2,000	12/31/16
Create community awareness	Develop branding/logo	Utilize professional resources that may be available both pro bono and paid	Approve brand/logo	Board	$1,000	6/30/17
Create community awareness	Develop website	Utilize professional resources that may be available both pro bono and paid	Approve website	Board	$2,000	8/30/17
Raise funds for construction of center	Establish goal and plan for raising money from public and private sources	Complete fundraising planning/feasibility study	Engage consultant	Development Committee/Board	$40,000	12/31/17
Raise funds for construction of center	Establish goal and plan for raising money from public and private sources	Complete fundraising planning/feasibility study	Develop list of potential interviewees	Development Committee/Consultant/Board	N/A	3/31/18
Raise funds for construction of center	Implement capital campaign	Utilize community volunteers and guidance of fundraising consultant	Engage consultant	Board	$80,000	4/30/19
Complete design and construction of center	Approve architectural and exhibit designs	Utilize research available	Review costs and findings from study	Board	$60,000	12/31/17
Develop plan for operation of center	Create staffing plan	Utilize research from successful museums	Develop a plan for staffing the center with paid staff and volunteers	Board/Project Director	N/A	1/31/18

See template for a board responsibility chart in **Appendix D**.

The planning cabinet can then review with the board where it stands on each area that was assigned to the board. Of course, it is sometimes difficult for a staff member to hold the board accountable, so it will be important to have at least one board member on the planning cabinet. The areas of responsibility should be reviewed at each meeting of the team responsible—whether it is the full board, a board committee, or a staff department.

Budget

Likewise you will want to monitor the revenue and expense items of the plan. The planning cabinet should review these items periodically with the chief financial officer and treasurer of the board. We suggest a monthly review of the budget at staff and board meetings.

> You may find it helpful to estimate the cost of each initiative by listing the related capital expenditures, startup and ongoing costs, and potential savings. This information will help you as you conduct your annual budgeting process.
>
> **Example**

Initiative 1

Capital Expenditures

Line Item	Estimated Cost	Purchase Period	Notes/Description
Subtotal: Capital expenditures	$		

Startup Costs

Line Item	Estimated Cost	Timing (When Costs Will Be Incurred)	Notes/Description
Subtotal: Startup costs	$		

Total capital expenditures and startup costs: $_____

Ongoing Costs

Line Item	Estimated Cost	Begin Date	Notes/Description
Subtotal: Ongoing costs	$		

Estimated Savings

Line Item	Estimated Savings	Savings Period (When Savings Are Due to Begin and End)	Notes/Description
Subtotal: Estimated savings	$		

Total annual operating cost (less savings): $_____

Timelines

The planning cabinet and/or chair of the planning cabinet will have the primary responsibility for making sure the plan gets implemented. In order to do that it will be helpful if, after the plan is completed, they have a complete timeline in chronological order. This way, a cabinet member or chair can contact each person/team responsible for activities to get a status report.

It will be important to remember what we said in the last chapter—"stuff" happens. And not everything is going to fall in line exactly the way it is outlined on the master timeline. But as long as the people responsible understand what caused the delays and what can be done to get back on track, the plan should go smoothly.

So What Happens When It Goes Astray?

As we've said, plans are not written in stone, but neither should they be written in disappearing ink! The reason you have benchmarks and monitoring of the plan is to make sure it actually does get implemented. Too often a lot of time and money is spent on developing a plan that no one follows (or sometimes even knows where the plan is). This is usually because there were too many goals, goals were unrealistic, action steps were not assigned to each objective, or no one took responsibility for monitoring the plan.

If you follow all the steps outlined in this manual, the plan will not go completely off track, although some things might fall through the cracks. So if an individual or a team is not completing its tasks, it is time to ask:

 ◆ Were the right people responsible for completing this task?

 ◆ Did we provide the individual or teams involved the right tools to complete their tasks?

 ◆ Were timelines and budgets realistic?

 ◆ Did external forces alter the chances of this goals being successfully implemented?

If one of these areas is the culprit for a task not getting implemented, how can you address the problem? One or more of these approaches might solve the problem:

 ◆ Reassign this task to another individual or team.

 ◆ Ask the individual or team involved if they understand the task assigned to them and how it fits into the plan.

Here is a sample of a master timeline that the planning cabinet should have in hand when monitoring the plan:

Sample Timeline for Annual Implementation

Decision Unit	August	September	October	November	December	January
Board			Quarterly strategic update			Kickoff planning
Executive Committee	Communicate annual plan					First planning meeting: ◆ Update/set annual goals ◆ Update/set annual initiatives
Management Team	Quarterly reviews			X		
Program/Operations Functions	Monthly program/operations reviews	X	X	X	X	X

Decision Unit	February	March	April	May	June	July
Board			Quarterly strategic update			Approve annual plan and budget
Executive Committee		Second planning meeting: ◆ Determine budget targets ◆ Review initiative metrics		Third planning meeting: ◆ Review detailed budgets		
Management Team	X			X	Align resources	
Program/Operations Functions	X	X	X Translate priorities into action plans	X Develop program/department annual budgets	X Update/set staffs annual goals	

Note: This timeline uses an August–July fiscal year.

◆ Talk to the individual or team responsible and ask if they need more time, more staff resources, more money, more information.

◆ Make the necessary adjustments to the budget, timeline, or person(s) responsible.

◆ If all else fails; reconsider if this task is appropriate for the objective, if the objective is needed in order to complete the goal, and if the goal is still realistic.

To Recap

◆ The planning cabinet is not responsible for implementing the entire plan, but is responsible for ensuring that individuals and teams responsible are on task.

◆ You need to have benchmarks in place to monitor the progress of the plan.

◆ When things go wrong, the planning cabinet should ask the individual and/or team what can be done to get back on track.

Chapter Fifteen

Planning for the Next Plan

IN THIS CHAPTER

- Begin the planning process for the next time period near the end of current planning period.

- Use evaluation of the current plan to strengthen the next plan.

- Remember to celebrate.

When you monitor and evaluate progress on implementation of the plan throughout the covered time period, you will gain valuable information to use in developing the next plan. As you reach the end of the current planning period, you'll want to closely review all steps in the development and implementation of the existing plan. That close look, a cooperative effort with board members and staff, will help you take advantage of what worked well and minimize the impact of what could have been better. You'll be on the right road to planning for the next plan.

Quick question: where is your nonprofit's strategic plan? Hopefully, you know where the plan is and that plan has been in constant use helping you make short-term and long-term decisions. You have "held the plan in your hand" as you grappled with fundraising options, program choices, and external communications.

Clarity is perhaps the single-most cited benefit of having a strategic plan. Your strategic plan (and the leaders who implemented the plan) most likely guided your organization to where it is today. Clarity on your mission, goals, and strategies eases the pressures of making quick decisions and choosing between options in a crisis.

Here's a scary thought—without clarity, an organization will be more likely to flounder. We can't underestimate the importance of having a clear direction and focus for your organization.

So, here you are in the last year of your three-year strategic plan. Do you have a tickler on your calendar about starting to plan for the next strategic planning process? Good for you! Now that is good planning.

Indicators That Can Signal the Need for a New Plan

While the timeline of your strategic plan provides a calendar showing when to start planning for your next strategic plan, you and your organization may be receiving some solid indicators that you should develop a new plan.

◆ Funding. Are there changes in the types and levels of support from your funders? Are funders expressing concern about the viability of your organization?

◆ Competition. Are there new competitors or potential collaborators entering the areas in which you've been operating? Are you seeing new and emerging program models that might create opportunities for you to provide services more efficiently and effectively?

◆ Policies. Are there new internal or external policies creating opportunities or challenges that will have an impact on what you can achieve as an organization?

◆ Leadership. Do you have a new CEO or executive director or a new and dramatic change in board leadership?

important

Remember our discussion in **Chapter Two** about planning to plan? As you start the last year of your current strategic plan, you may find it helpful to bring your planning committee together to take close look at where you are in your strategic plan and where you want to go.

We noted that the one thing all good plans have in common is that the people developing the plan were focused and committed to creating a plan that would work. So, as you have traveled the strategic planning journey, we feel certain that your starts and stops along the way have been different and unique to your organization. And, while your strategic planning journeys appear quite different, the thing you and most organizations have in common is that those journeys—your strategic planning—are both a process and a product.

As you prepare for your next strategic planning, take a glance back. Truthfully, you'll need a little more than a glance. Review your process and how you developed the current plan. Did it work for you? Did it meet your needs? Did you have enough resources to handle the process? Did you engage the staff and board? Perhaps some people involved in one stage of the process might be better suited to other tasks at other stages of the process.

What Will Your Next Planning Process Look Like?

Since you already have a strategic plan in place, your planning process should begin with a review of the existing plan to determine which goals have been completed, which ones are still valid, and which are no longer pertinent.

Did you use a SWOT analysis for the existing plan? If so, will you re-assess your internal strengths and weaknesses and your external opportunities and threats as part of the process for your next strategic plan? Great idea! A comparison of the two results can give you some interesting insights into your progress.

Did you work with a consultant or facilitator to develop your current plan? How did that work for you? Are you now confident in the process and ready to oversee the process yourselves? Those are key questions you will need to consider as you design your next planning process.

Evaluation Can Strengthen Your Next Plan

A major part of the evaluation of your strategic plan includes a determination of how well the plan has been implemented. You will review who, what, when, where, and how activities were accomplished. Your planning cabinet will monitor progress on the plan, however, the board or a committee of the board should oversee evaluation of the plan.

Ideally, the planning cabinet has been meeting quarterly to monitor progress on the plan. In tandem, the executive director and staff have implemented work plans aligned with the plan's goals and objectives and those plans are progressing well and on target.

The ongoing monitoring effort should focus on these questions:

◆ Are activities being implemented as planned?

◆ Did all activities fit within the objectives of the plan?

◆ Are some goal areas, objectives, or strategies receiving less attention than others?

◆ How can we improve the results?

◆ Do we need to change the plan?

If the plan changes, ensure that you manage the various versions of the plan and include a new date on each new version of the plan. Always keep old copies of the plan.

In addition to the periodic and ongoing monitoring, you will want to take a final look and evaluate the success and impact of the plan upon its completion or at the end of the planning period.

You may choose to appoint a special Strategic Plan Evaluation Task Force or board committee to complete the final report or this task can be performed by the planning cabinet.

Questions to ask in the final evaluation:

◆ How well did the plan perform? What did we do as a result of this plan? Which goals and objectives did we accomplish? What actions did we successfully implement?

◆ How well did we do as an organization in following our plan? Were the goals and objectives relevant to the needs of our organization?

◆ What is the impact of this strategic plan? Did the plan meet the needs of our organization and its stakeholders?

Once the planning cabinet or board committee has gathered information related to these questions, they should prepare a report organized by goal area. For each goal area, they can outline ongoing and completed accomplishments and include feedback from board and staff members. The report should also provide a summary of progress on objectives and a profile of challenges and successes.

As part of the evaluation and reporting process, you will want to encourage discussion and be sure to write down what you have learned from the current planning activity to make the next strategic planning activity more efficient.

We Did It

If you watch the children's television series *Dora the Explorer*, you know that each successful adventure she and her trusty friend Boots complete, they celebrate with a rousing rendition of a song entitled *"We Did It."* And, of course, they are always successful.

Very rarely do organizations take the time to truly acknowledge the success they have achieved when they complete a plan. Instead of taking the time to celebrate, planners focus too much on progress and problem-solving and eagerly move on to the next version of the plan.

So you completed the plan. Stop. Celebrate. Celebration is just as important as accomplishing objectives and maybe more so. You can generate even more enthusiasm for the next planning cycle by spreading a sense of fulfillment and closure. Acknowledge cheerfully the work of participants in a job well done and celebrate!

Then, you are ready to begin work on your next plan.

To Recap

◆ Begin planning for your next strategic plan as you near the end of your current planning period.

◆ Ongoing monitoring and evaluation helps you identify trends that might have an impact on the progress on the plan.

◆ The final report on the plan should outline ongoing and completed accomplishments and provide a profile of challenges and successes.

Appendix A

Sample Plan

Northwest Vista College Strategic Plan 2010–2015
Revised 2012

Reprinted with permission from Northwest Vista College

Objective I

Completion: In order to support our students and community, we provide college-wide support for completion.

Strategy I.A. Support Underrepresented Populations. Improve support programs and processes for underrepresented populations that lead to completion (target Hispanics, African Americans, returning adults).

Organization Action Plan (OAP) I.A.1. Recruitment and Retention Programs and Processes. Create and strengthen programs and processes to enroll and retain students from underrepresented populations.

1. *Financial aid.* strengthen services for students including improved communication, training, information, intervention strategies.

2. *Improve student access to services.* transcript services and phone processes.

3. *Contact potential leavers.* Contact current students who have not enrolled by priority registration.

Strategy I.B. Degree Completion. Develop infrastructure and services to support students from pre-enrollment to certificate and degree completion and/or transfer.

OAP I.B.1. Developmental Education to Degree Completion. Prepare students for degree and certificate completion and develop infrastructure to support degree and certificate completion.

1. *Developmental education.* Improve testing for placement in DE and accelerate students through courses; improve advising for DE students.

2. *Staff/faculty advising.* Implement a shared staff/ faculty advising model for academic and workforce career programs.

3. *Promoting degree completion.* Develop and implement systems and activities that focus on degree completion.

OAP I.B.2. Workforce Certificate/Degree Completion. Develop a stronger career planning and workforce placement model that includes student tracking.

1. Improve the current Workforce students' tracking database to ensure accurate data is collected on completers and placement of such upon graduation.

OAP I. B.3. Foundations of Excellence. Focus on FTIC through this national partnership.

1. *Self-study.* Engage the campus in data to find focus for improvement in completion.

2. *Student development (SDev).* Address and improve student learning outcomes; improve faculty development and learning communities; focus on degree planning and completion. Integrate plans with faculty advising.

3. *New student orientation.* Make early connections with new students.

Objective II

Learning: We enhance engagement, success, and learning for all.

Strategy II.A. Learning Quality and Effectiveness. Enhance curriculum and teaching and learning models to improve student learning outcomes.

OAP II.A.1. Learning Outcomes. Measure, review and Improve Student Learning Outcomes by discipline and program (academic and student success). Identify SLOs, develop assessment plans, carry out evaluations, and implement improvements.

    1a. *Academic discipline learning outcomes.* Programs to align student learning outcomes. Identify SLOs, develop assessment plans, carry out evaluations, and implement improvements.

    1b. *Workforce discipline learning outcomes.* Programs to align student learning outcomes.

2. *Student success learning outcomes.* Each area will identify student learning outcomes.

OAP II.A.2. Distance learning. Improve distance learning success and retention through evaluation, support services and faculty development. (2011)

1. *Online high-risk courses.* Develop an evaluation that identifies high risk courses; for each high risk course determine root cause and develop strategies for improvement.

2. *Improve student support services online* (e.g., Hola, Boldchat, Degree Works, CAMS) and other services).

OAP II.A.3. Interdisciplinary Programs. Grow and strengthen Interdisciplinary programs.

1. *Develop and implement core to core learning communities.*

2. *Honors' program.* Identify additional faculty to work on this initiative, develop a plan that re-invents the focus of program.

3. *Service learning.* Task force to develop and/or expand service learning goals and initiatives.

4. *Peace and conflict studies.* Develop a module on conflict management and resolution to incorporate into the core curriculum (Determine where in the core) Mexican American Studies.

5. *Prepare students for college-level instruction and success* through Student Development Courses, co-curricular programs (ambassadors, etc.).

OAP II.A.4. Workforce Program Plan. Expand the number of Workforce Programs.

OAP II.A.5. Community Education. Assess and expand community education programs based on return on investment and community needs.

Strategy II.B. Employee Learning and Engagement. Enhance critical communication flow processes, employee development and evaluation system, and college culture to assure employee effectiveness, engagement, and learning.

OAP II.B.1. Faculty Development and Staff Development. Enhance employee development to engage all faculty and staff members. Expand developmental education orientation model to all faculty (share Information on model).

1. *Strengthen and expand faculty orientation model* used by Developmental Education faculty.

2. *Increase faculty development offerings online.* Improve and Implement on-line training and resources. Identify a timeline for E-Team input and another timeline for implementation.

3. *Increase staff development offerings*, including those online.

4. *Create faculty and staff development requirements* to include number of hours required each year and any other specific requirements.

OAP II.B.2. Valuing Diversity. Develop and Implement training in valuing diversity

OAP II.B.3. Conflict Resolution. Infuse conflict management training across college.

OAP II.B.4. Leadership Cultivation. Create employee evaluation and development models that tie to succession planning.

1. *Prepare employees for leadership positions* through Leadership Development Team.

2. *Leadership lab.* develop promising leaders and assess next steps move to Leadership Lab II.

Objective III

Sustainability: We develop sustainability models to support the NVC Vision.

Strategy III.A. Financial Sustainability. Maximize the effective use of current resources.

OAP III.A.1. Assess Resources. Assess resource availability and usage required to meet needed operational effectiveness, including human, technical, facilities, and financial resources.

1. *Assess capacity to serve* including resources and identify and fill resource gaps.

OAP III.A.2. Return on Investment. Develop models and assess strategic alignment of budget and cost effectiveness of programs and services.

OAP III.A.3. Generate New Sources of Revenues.

1. *Provide funding* through Federal and other grants.

2. *Develop infrastructure* to support use of facilities to generate revenue.

3. *Foundation fundraising.* Increase revenues for operations and scholarships from Foundation fundraising. Develop cycle of activities that heightens the awareness of NVC in the community.

Strategy III.B. Community and Partnership Development. Develop community partnerships that sustain the college and support student success.

OAP III.B.1. Engage Community Partners.

Strategy III.C. Internal Relationships. Create new opportunities for effective employee and district interaction and communication.

OAP III.C.1. Culture and Communication. Alamo Community Colleges District intervention—collaborate/intervene

Appendix B

Planning Tools

Roles and Responsibilities in Strategic Planning

Stakeholders	Responsibilities
Planning process champion	Believes in strategic planning and helps keep the planning process on track
Board of Directors	Approves the strategic plan and monitors performance
Planning Cabinet or Leadership Group	Oversees process, makes final decisions regarding plan decision
Plan Writer	Takes notes during planning meetings and uses them to prepare the plan
Staff	Provides input regarding implementation
Other constituent groups	Provide perspectives and input regarding the community and environment
Clients	Those who benefit from the organization's services are sometimes involved in the planning process
Planning process facilitator	Plans each meeting's agenda and ensures the group stays on track

Components of a Written Strategic Plan

Element	Description	What Does it Answer?
Mission	A statement describing an organization's core purpose or reason for being	Why do we stop?
Vision	A statement describing an organization's desired future position	Where are we going and where do we want to end up?
Values/Guiding Principles	Beliefs an organization lives by and cherishes above all others	What shapes our actions?

Element	Description	What Does it Answer?
Strategic Direction	Longer-term direction that this plan makes progress in achieving	Where are we going in the foreseeable longer term?
Goals	The end results we seek to accomplish through our efforts	What do we need to focus on to reach our vision?
Measures of Success	Measures and targets indicating desired outcomes and illustrating progress	How do we know if we are successful in achieving our vision or goals?
Strategies	Specific plans for deploying resources to reach a favorable and desired position and achieve goals	What projects or activities are necessary to reach our goals?

Strategic Planning Process Chart

Process Phases and Associated Tasks

Check when complete.

Getting Started, Designing, Assessing	√	Setting a Vision	√	Defining Goals	√	Integration and Plan Adoption	√
Planning cabinet outlines planning issues		Data is collected		Work groups assigned		Planning cabinet reviews draft of plan	
Planning cabinet determines data sources		Data is analyzed		Work groups develop action plans		Board reviews and adopts plan	
Board and staff develop data collection strategy		Planning cabinet meets to review data analysis and plan retreat		Work groups name resource needed		Communication plan developed to explain priorities	
Planning roles and responsibilities identified		Board, staff and others meet in retreat		Planning cabinet meets to review work group reports and set priorities		Implementation begins	

Appendix C

Sample Benchmarking

(See next page.)

Benchmarking by Areas of Responsibility: Board of Directors

Goal	Objective	Strategy	Action Steps	Responsibility	Budget	Timeline
Create Community Awareness	Develop and implement marketing plan	Utilize professional resources that may be available both pro bono and paid	Approve plan	Board		
Create Community Awareness	Develop Branding/ Logo	Utilize professional resources that may be available both pro bono and paid	Approve brand/logo	Board		
Create Community Awareness	Develop website	Utilize professional resources that may be available both pro bono and paid	Approve website	Board		
Raise Funds for Construction of Center	Establish goal and plan for raising money from public and private sources	Complete fundraising planning /feasibility study	Engage consultant	Development Committee/ Board		
Raise Funds for Construction of Center	Establish goal and plan for raising money from public and private sources	Complete fundraising planning /feasibility study	Develop list of potential interviewees	Development Committee/ Consultant/ Board		
Raise Funds for Construction of Center	Implement capital campaign	Utilize community volunteers and guidance of fundraising consultant	Engage consultant	Board		
Complete Design and Construction of Center	Approve architectural and exhibit designs	Utilize research available	Review costs and findings from study	Board		
Develop Plan for Operation of Center	Create staffing plan	Utilize research from successful museums	Develop a plan for staffing the Center with paid staff and volunteers	Board/Project Director		

Benchmarking by Areas of Responsibility: Board Resource/Governance Committee

Goal	Objective	Strategy	Action Steps	Responsibility	Budget	Timeline
Develop Plan for Operation of Center	Create board development plan	Utilize staff and consultant expertise	Develop a plan for ongoing board development including diversifying the board geographically, ethnically, etc.	Board Resource/ Governance Committee		

Benchmarking by Areas of Responsibility: Building Committee

Goal	Objective	Strategy	Action Steps	Responsibility	Budget	Timeline
Raise Funds for Construction of Center	Establish goal and plan for raising money from public and private sources	Complete fundraising planning /feasibility study	Provide consultants with drawing and information for case for support	Building Committee		
Determine Feasibility if Interim Facility	Determine feasibility of securing temporary facility	Utilize partnership opportunities	Develop a recommendation based on findings of building committee and program committee	Program Committee/ Building Committee		
Determine Feasibility if Interim Facility	Determine feasibility of traveling or modular facility	Utilize partnership opportunities	Develop a recommendation based on findings of building committee and program committee	Program Committee/ Building Committee		
Complete Design and Construction of Center	Finalize site development plan	Utilize construction professionals and staff expertise	Engage site developers	Building Committee		

Benchmarking by Areas of Responsibility: Communications Committee

Goal	Objective	Strategy	Action Steps	Responsibility	Budget	Timeline
Create Community Awareness	Develop and implement marketing plan	Utilize professional resources that may be available both pro bono and paid	Determine what assistance is available from City of Henderson/possible students at Art Institute or UNLV/College of Southern NV	Communications Committee		
Create Community Awareness	Develop and implement marketing plan	Utilize professional resources that may be available both pro bono and paid	Develop plan	Communications Committee		
Create Community Awareness	Develop Branding/ Logo	Utilize professional resources that may be available both pro bono and paid	Determine what assistance is available from City of Henderson/possible students at Art Institute or UNLV/ College of Southern NV	Communications Committee		
Create Community Awareness	Develop website	Utilize professional resources that may be available both pro bono and paid	Determine what assistance is available from City of Henderson/possible students at Art Institute or UNLV/ College of Southern NV	Communications Committee		
Create Community Awareness	Develop appropriate marketing materials for outreach	Work with program committee	Develop list of partners and appropriate materials for various audiences	Communications Committee/ Marketing Consultant or Student		

Goal	Objective	Strategy	Action Steps	Responsibility	Budget	Timeline
Create Community Awareness	Develop appropriate marketing materials for outreach	Work with program committee	Approve materials and produce	Communications Committee		
Create Community Awareness	Develop appropriate marketing materials for capital campaign	Review case for support developed by campaign consultant	Develop materials for capital campaign	Communications Committee/Campaign Consultant		
Create Community Awareness	Develop appropriate marketing materials for capital campaign	Review case for support developed by campaign consultant	Approve materials and produce	Campaign Cabinet/Communications Committee		
Create Community Awareness	Develop appropriate marketing materials for completed center (both program and fundraising)	Work with development/marketing staff or consultants; review case for support prepared for Center operations	Develop materials for fundraising from case	Communications Committee/Development Staff		

Benchmarking by Areas of Responsibility: Consultants/Outside Contractors

Goal	Objective	Strategy	Action Steps	Responsibility	Budget	Timeline
Create Community Awareness	Develop Branding/Logo	Utilize professional resources that may be available both pro bono and paid	Develop brand/logo	Marketing Consultant or Student		
Create Community Awareness	Develop website	Utilize professional resources that may be available both pro bono and paid	Develop website	Marketing Consultant or Student		
Create Community Awareness	Develop appropriate marketing materials for outreach	Work with program committee	Develop list of partners and appropriate materials for various audiences	Communications Committee/Marketing Consultant or Student		

Goal	Objective	Strategy	Action Steps	Responsibility	Budget	Timeline
Create Community Awareness	Develop appropriate marketing materials for capital campaign	Review case for support developed by campaign consultant	Develop materials for capital campaign	Communications Committee/ Campaign Consultant		
Raise Funds for Construction of Center	Establish goal and plan for raising money from public and private sources	Complete fundraising planning /feasibility study	Develop list of potential interviewees	Development Committee/ Consultant/ Board		
Raise Funds for Construction of Center	Establish goal and plan for raising money from public and private sources	Complete fundraising planning /feasibility study	Develop preliminary case, conduct internal assessment and interviews, prepare report	Consultant		
Raise Funds for Construction of Center	Implement capital campaign	Consultant to develop plan	Develop campaign plan	Campaign Consultant		
Raise Funds for Construction of Center	Implement capital campaign	Key community leaders identified in study	Recruit campaign leadership	Development Committee/ Consultant		
Raise Funds for Construction of Center	Secure government funding	Utilize a variety of sources of government funding, leveraging private fundraising campaign	Investigate federal, state and local opportunities for funding	Development Committee/ Volunteer/ Outside Grant Contractor		
Raise Funds for Construction of Center	Secure government funding	Utilize a variety of sources of government funding, leveraging private fundraising campaign	Write grant proposals as appropriate	Volunteer/ Outside Grant Contractor		
Complete Design and Construction of Center	Create building design	Utilize construction professionals and staff expertise	Plans and renderings	Architect		
Complete Design and Construction of Center	Construction of Center	Utilize construction professionals and staff expertise	Break ground, commence construction	Architect/ Construction Company		

Benchmarking by Areas of Responsibility: Development Committee

Goal	Objective	Strategy	Action Steps	Responsibility	Budget	Timeline
Raise Funds for Construction of Center	Establish goal and plan for raising money from public and private sources	Complete fundraising planning /feasibility study	Engage consultant	Development Committee/ Board		
Raise Funds for Construction of Center	Establish goal and plan for raising money from public and private sources	Complete fundraising planning /feasibility study	Develop list of potential interviewees	Development Committee/ Consultant/ Board		
Raise Funds for Construction of Center	Implement capital campaign	Key community leaders identified in study	Recruit campaign leadership	Development Committee/ Consultant		
Raise Funds for Construction of Center	Secure government funding	Utilize a variety of sources of government funding , leveraging private fundraising campaign	Investigate federal, state and local opportunities for funding	Development Committee/ Volunteer/ Outside Grant Contractor		

Benchmarking by Areas of Responsibility: Finance Committee

Goal	Objective	Strategy	Action Steps	Responsibility	Budget	Timeline
Develop Plan for Operation of Center	Create budget	Utilize staff and consultant expertise	Develop a three year operating budget	Finance Committee/ Project Director		

Benchmarking by Areas of Responsibility: Program Committee

Goal	Objective	Strategy	Action Steps	Responsibility	Budget	Timeline
Develop Strong Programs	Develop programs to be operated before Center is open	Engage partners and develop collaborative opportunities	Develop list of potential partners (schools/other museums, etc.	Program Committee		

Goal	Objective	Strategy	Action Steps	Responsibility	Budget	Timeline
Develop Strong Programs	Develop programs to be operated before Center is open	Engage partners and develop collaborative opportunities	Develop program schedule for next three years while construction is being completed	Program Committee		
Develop Strong Programs	Develop programs to be operated in Center	Utilize professional skills of staff, volunteers and outside consultants	Develop on site and off site program schedule for first 3 years of operation	Program Committee		
Determine Feasibility if Interim Facility	Determine feasibility of securing temporary facility	Utilize partnership opportunities	Develop a recommendation based on findings of building committee and program committee	Program Committee/ Building Committee		
Determine Feasibility if Interim Facility	Determine feasibility of traveling or modular facility	Utilize partnership opportunities	Develop a recommendation based on findings of building committee and program committee	Program Committee/ Building Committee		

Benchmarking by Areas of Responsibility: Staff

Goal	Objective	Strategy	Action Steps	Responsibility	Budget	Timeline
Create Community Awareness	Develop appropriate marketing materials for completed center (both program and fundraising)	Work with development/ marketing staff or consultants; review case for support prepared for Center operations	Approve materials and produce	Development Staff		
Complete Design and Construction of Center	Develop exhibit plan	Utilize professional exhibit design firm and staff expertise	Contact exhibit design firms	Project Director		

Goal	Objective	Strategy	Action Steps	Responsibility	Budget	Timeline
Develop Plan for Operation of Center	Create program plan	Utilize research from successful museums	Develop a plan for first three year programming	Program Staff		
Develop Plan for Operation of Center	Create staffing plan	Utilize research from successful museums	Develop a plan for staffing the Center with paid staff and volunteers	Board/Project Director		
Develop Plan for Operation of Center	Create development plan	Utilize staff and consultant expertise	Develop plan for annual operating income, endowment income suing planned giving techniques, grants and special events	Development Director		
Develop Plan for Operation of Center	Create marketing plan	Utilize staff and consultant expertise	Develop a plan for marketing the Center's program, events and activities	Marketing Director		
Develop Plan for Operation of Center	Create budget	Utilize staff and consultant expertise	Develop a three year operating budget	Finance Committee/ Project Director		

Benchmarking by Areas of Responsibility: Volunteers

Goal	Objective	Strategy	Action Steps	Responsibility	Budget	Timeline
Create Community Awareness	Develop Branding/ Logo	Utilize professional resources that may be available both pro bono and paid	Develop brand/logo	Marketing Consultant or Student		
Create Community Awareness	Develop website	Utilize professional resources that may be available both pro bono and paid	Develop website	Marketing Consultant or Student		

Goal	Objective	Strategy	Action Steps	Responsibility	Budget	Timeline
Create Community Awareness	Develop appropriate marketing materials for outreach	Work with program committee	Develop list of partners and appropriate materials for various audiences	Communications Committee/ Marketing Consultant or Student		
Raise Funds for Construction of Center	Implement capital campaign	Capital campaign best practices	Launch campaign	Campaign Cabinet		
Raise Funds for Construction of Center	Secure government funding	Utilize a variety of sources of government funding, leveraging private fundraising campaign	Investigate federal, state and local opportunities for funding	Development Committee/ Volunteer/ Outside Grant Contractor		
Raise Funds for Construction of Center	Secure government funding	Utilize a variety of sources of government funding, leveraging private fundraising campaign	Write grant proposals as appropriate	Volunteer/ Outside Grant Contractor		

Example of a Board Responsibilities Benchmarking Chart

Benchmarking by Areas of Responsibility: Board of Directors

Goal	Objective	Strategy	Action Steps	Responsibility	Budget	Timeline
Create Community Awareness	Develop and implement marketing plan	Utilize professional resources that may be available both pro bono and paid	Approve plan	Board	$2,000	12/31/15
Create Community Awareness	Develop Branding/ Logo	Utilize professional resources that may be available both pro bono and paid	Approve brand/logo	Board	$1,000	6/30/16
Create Community Awareness	Develop website	Utilize professional resources that may be available both pro bono and paid	Approve website	Board	$2,000	8/31/16

Goal	Objective	Strategy	Action Steps	Responsibility	Budget	Timeline
Raise Funds for Construction of Center	Establish goal and plan for raising money from public and private sources	Complete fundraising planning/feasibility study	Engage consultant	Development Committee/Board	$40,000	12/31/16
Raise Funds for Construction of Center	Establish goal and plan for raising money from public and private sources	Complete fundraising planning/feasibility study	Develop list of potential interviewees	Development Committee/Consultant/Board	N/A	3/31/17
Raise Funds for Construction of Center	Implement capital campaign	Utilize community volunteers and guidance of fundraising consultant	Engage consultant	Board	$80,000	4/30/18
Complete Design and Construction of Center	Approve architectural and exhibit designs	Utilize research available	Review costs and findings from study	Board	$60,000	12/31/16
Develop Plan for Operation of Center	Create staffing plan	Utilize research from successful museums	Develop a plan for staffing the Center with paid staff and volunteers	Board/Project Director	N/A	1/31/17

Benchmarking by Areas of Responsibility: Board Resource/Governance Committee

Goal	Objective	Strategy	Action Steps	Responsibility	Budget	Timeline
Develop Plan for Operation of Center	Create board development plan	Utilize staff and consultant expertise	Develop a plan for ongoing board development including diversifying the board geographically, ethnically, etc.	Board Resource/Governance Committee	N/A	12/31/16

Benchmarking by Areas of Responsibility: Building Committee

Goal	Objective	Strategy	Action Steps	Responsibility	Budget	Timeline
Raise Funds for Construction of Center	Establish goal and plan for raising money from public and private sources	Complete fundraising planning/feasibility study	Provide consultants with drawing and information for case for support	Building Committee		

Goal	Objective	Strategy	Action Steps	Responsibility	Budget	Timeline
Determine Feasibility if Interim Facility	Determine feasibility of securing temporary facility	Utilize partnership opportunities	Develop a recommendation based on findings of building committee and program committee	Program Committee/ Building Committee		
Determine Feasibility if Interim Facility	Determine feasibility of traveling or modular facility	Utilize partnership opportunities	Develop a recommendation based on findings of building committee and program committee	Program Committee/ Building Committee		
Complete Design and Construction of Center	Finalize site development plan	Utilize construction professionals and staff expertise	Engage site developers	Building Committee		

Benchmarking by Areas of Responsibility: Communications Committee

Goal	Objective	Strategy	Action Steps	Responsibility	Budget	Timeline
Create Community Awareness	Develop and implement marketing plan	Utilize professional resources that may be available both pro bono and paid	Determine what assistance is available from City of Henderson/possible students at Art Institute or UNLV/College of Southern NV	Communications Committee		
Create Community Awareness	Develop and implement marketing plan	Utilize professional resources that may be available both pro bono and paid	Develop plan	Communications Committee		
Create Community Awareness	Develop Branding/ Logo	Utilize professional resources that may be available both pro bono and paid	Determine what assistance is available from City of Henderson/possible students at Art Institute or UNLV/College of Southern NV	Communications Committee		

Goal	Objective	Strategy	Action Steps	Responsibility	Budget	Timeline
Create Community Awareness	Develop website	Utilize professional resources that may be available both pro bono and paid	Determine what assistance is available from City of Henderson/ possible students at Art Institute or UNLV/College of Southern NV	Communications Committee		
Create Community Awareness	Develop appropriate marketing materials for outreach	Work with program committee	Develop list of partners and appropriate materials for various audiences	Communications Committee/ Marketing Consultant or Student		
Create Community Awareness	Develop appropriate marketing materials for outreach	Work with program committee	Approve materials and produce	Communications Committee		
Create Community Awareness	Develop appropriate marketing materials for capital campaign	Review case for support developed by campaign consultant	Develop materials for capital campaign	Communications Committee/ Campaign Consultant		
Create Community Awareness	Develop appropriate marketing materials for capital campaign	Review case for support developed by campaign consultant	Approve materials and produce	Campaign Cabinet/ Communications Committee		
Create Community Awareness	Develop appropriate marketing materials for completed center (both program and fundraising)	Work with development/ marketing staff or consultants; review case for support prepared for Center operations	Develop materials for fundraising from case	Communications Committee/ Development Staff		

Benchmarking by Areas of Responsibility: Consultants/Outside Contractors

Goal	Objective	Strategy	Action Steps	Responsibility	Budget	Timeline
Create Community Awareness	Develop Branding/Logo	Utilize professional resources that may be available both pro bono and paid	Develop brand/logo	Marketing Consultant or Student		
Create Community Awareness	Develop website	Utilize professional resources that may be available both pro bono and paid	Develop website	Marketing Consultant or Student		
Create Community Awareness	Develop appropriate marketing materials for outreach	Work with program committee	Develop list of partners and appropriate materials for various audiences	Communications Committee/ Marketing Consultant or Student		
Create Community Awareness	Develop appropriate marketing materials for capital campaign	Review case for support developed by campaign consultant	Develop materials for capital campaign	Communications Committee/ Campaign Consultant		
Raise Funds for Construction of Center	Establish goal and plan for raising money from public and private sources	Complete fundraising planning /feasibility study	Develop list of potential interviewees	Development Committee/ Consultant/ Board		
Raise Funds for Construction of Center	Establish goal and plan for raising money from public and private sources	Complete fundraising planning /feasibility study	Develop preliminary case, conduct internal assessment and interviews, prepare report	Consultant		
Raise Funds for Construction of Center	Implement capital campaign	Consultant to develop plan	Develop campaign plan	Campaign Consultant		
Raise Funds for Construction of Center	Implement capital campaign	Key community leaders identified in study	Recruit campaign leadership	Development Committee/ Consultant		

Goal	Objective	Strategy	Action Steps	Responsibility	Budget	Timeline
Raise Funds for Construction of Center	Secure government funding	Utilize a variety of sources of government funding, leveraging private fundraising campaign	Investigate federal, state and local opportunities for funding	Development Committee/ Volunteer/ Outside Grant Contractor		
Raise Funds for Construction of Center	Secure government funding	Utilize a variety of sources of government funding, leveraging private fundraising campaign	Write grant proposals as appropriate	Volunteer/ Outside Grant Contractor		
Complete Design and Construction of Center	Create building design	Utilize construction professionals and staff expertise	Plans and renderings	Architect		
Complete Design and Construction of Center	Construction of Center	Utilize construction professionals and staff expertise	Break ground, commence construction	Architect/ Construction Company		

Benchmarking by Areas of Responsibility: Development Committee

Goal	Objective	Strategy	Action Steps	Responsibility	Budget	Timeline
Raise Funds for Construction of Center	Establish goal and plan for raising money from public and private sources	Complete fundraising planning /feasibility study	Engage consultant	Development Committee/ Board		
Raise Funds for Construction of Center	Establish goal and plan for raising money from public and private sources	Complete fundraising planning /feasibility study	Develop list of potential interviewees	Development Committee/ Consultant/ Board		
Raise Funds for Construction of Center	Implement capital campaign	Key community leaders identified in study	Recruit campaign leadership	Development Committee/ Consultant		
Raise Funds for Construction of Center	Secure government funding	Utilize a variety of sources of government funding, leveraging private fundraising campaign	Investigate federal, state and local opportunities for funding	Development Committee/ Volunteer/ Outside Grant Contractor		

Benchmarking by Areas of Responsibility: Finance Committee

Goal	Objective	Strategy	Action Steps	Responsibility	Budget	Timeline
Develop Plan for Operation of Center	Create budget	Utilize staff and consultant expertise	Develop a three year operating budget	Finance Committee/ Project Director		

Benchmarking by Areas of Responsibility: Program Committee

Goal	Objective	Strategy	Action Steps	Responsibility	Budget	Timeline
Develop Strong Programs	Develop programs to be operated before Center is open	Engage partners and develop collaborative opportunities	Develop list of potential partners (schools/other museums, etc.)	Program Committee		
Develop Strong Programs	Develop programs to be operated before Center is open	Engage partners and develop collaborative opportunities	Develop program schedule for next three years while construction is being completed	Program Committee		
Develop Strong Programs	Develop programs to be operated in Center	Utilize professional skills of staff, volunteers and outside consultants	Develop on site and off site program schedule for first 3 years of operation	Program Committee		
Determine Feasibility if Interim Facility	Determine feasibility of securing temporary facility	Utilize partnership opportunities	Develop a recommendation based on findings of building committee and program committee	Program Committee/ Building Committee		
Determine Feasibility if Interim Facility	Determine feasibility of traveling or modular facility	Utilize partnership opportunities	Develop a recommendation based on findings of building committee and program committee	Program Committee/ Building Committee		

Benchmarking by Areas of Responsibility: Staff

Goal	Objective	Strategy	Action Steps	Responsibility	Budget	Timeline
Create Community Awareness	Develop appropriate marketing materials for completed center (both program and fundraising)	Work with development/ marketing staff or consultants; review case for support prepared for Center operations	Approve materials and produce	Development Staff		
Complete Design and Construction of Center	Develop exhibit plan	Utilize professional exhibit design firm and staff expertise	Contact exhibit design firms	Project Director		
Develop Plan for Operation of Center	Create program plan	Utilize research from successful museums	Develop a plan for first three year programming	Program Staff		
Develop Plan for Operation of Center	Create staffing plan	Utilize research from successful museums	Develop a plan for staffing the Center with paid staff and volunteers	Board/Project Director		
Develop Plan for Operation of Center	Create development plan	Utilize staff and consultant expertise	Develop plan for annual operating income, endowment income suing planned giving techniques, grants and special events	Development Director		
Develop Plan for Operation of Center	Create marketing plan	Utilize staff and consultant expertise	Develop a plan for marketing the Center's program, events and activities	Marketing Director		
Develop Plan for Operation of Center	Create budget	Utilize staff and consultant expertise	Develop a three year operating budget	Finance Committee/ Project Director		

Benchmarking by Areas of Responsibility: Volunteers

Goal	Objective	Strategy	Action Steps	Responsibility	Budget	Timeline
Create Community Awareness	Develop Branding/Logo	Utilize professional resources that may be available both pro bono and paid	Develop brand/logo	Marketing Consultant or Student		
Create Community Awareness	Develop website	Utilize professional resources that may be available both pro bono and paid	Develop website	Marketing Consultant or Student		
Create Community Awareness	Develop appropriate marketing materials for outreach	Work with program committee	Develop list of partners and appropriate materials for various audiences	Communications Committee/ Marketing Consultant or Student		
Raise Funds for Construction of Center	Implement capital campaign	Capital campaign best practices	Launch campaign	Campaign Cabinet		
Raise Funds for Construction of Center	Secure government funding	Utilize a variety of sources of government funding, leveraging private fundraising campaign	Investigate federal, state and local opportunities for funding	Development Committee/ Volunteer/ Outside Grant Contractor		
Raise Funds for Construction of Center	Secure government funding	Utilize a variety of sources of government funding, leveraging private fundraising campaign	Write grant proposals as appropriate	Volunteer/ Outside Grant Contractor		

Appendix D

Templates

Working Planning Grid

Goal	Objective	Strategy	Budget	Responsibility	Completion Date

Goals and Objectives Grid

Goals, Objectives, Tasks	Responsibility Of	Anticipated Expense	Start Date	End Date
Goal				
Objective				
Task				
Objective Anticipated Income/Expense				
Objective				
Task				
Objective Anticipated Income/Expenses				

Strategic Plan Goals and Objectives

Goal	Objective	Strategy	Budget	Responsibility	Timeline

Benchmarking Plan by Area of Responsibility

Goal	Objective	Strategy	Action Steps	Responsibility	Budget	Timeline
				Board		

Goal	Objective	Strategy	Action Steps	Responsibility	Budget	Timeline
				Development Committee/Board		
				Board Resource/ Governance Committee		
				Building Committee		
				Communications Committee		
				Consultants/ Outside Contractors		
				Development Committee		
				Finance Committee		
				Program Committee		

Goal	Objective	Strategy	Action Steps	Responsibility	Budget	Timeline

Board Responsibility Chart

Goal	Objective	Strategy	Action Steps	Responsibility	Budget	Timeline
1				Board		
2						
3						

Index

If you enjoyed this manual, you'll want to pick up the other books in the CharityChannel Press **In the Trenches**™ series.

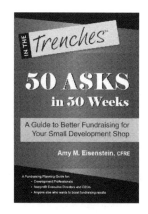

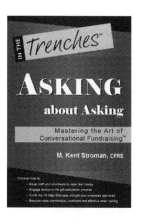
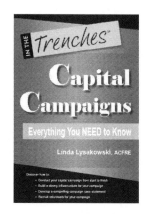
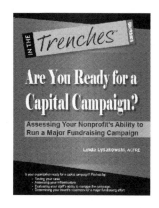

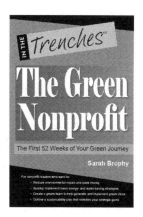
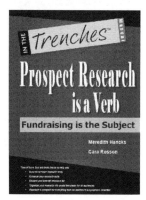

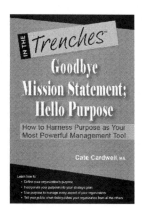
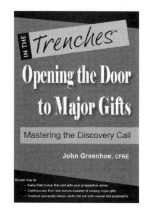

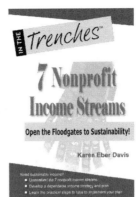

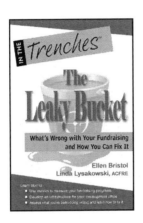

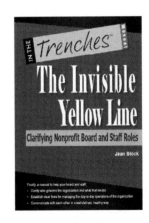

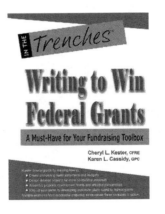
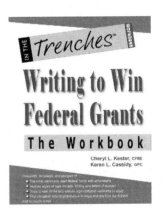

And now introducing **For the GENIUS® Press,** producing books on just about any topic that people want to learn. *You don't have to be a genius to read a GENIUS book, but you'll sure be smarter once you do!*™

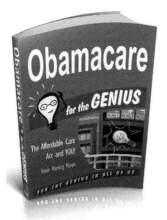

And more!

ForTheGENIUS.com/bookstore

Made in the USA
Columbia, SC
11 October 2020